Visual

Facebook

For Everyone

Marcel C. Obi, Ph.D.

KTA Publishing

Visual Facebook For Everyone

By Dr. Marcel C. Obi

Copyright © 2014 Marcel C. Obi. All rights reserved
Printed in the United States of America

Published by
KTA Publishing.www.kommo-academy.com
P. O. Box 4101, Cerritos, CA 90703

Graphics, Layout and Designs: Dr. Marcel C. Obi
Indexer: Microsoft Word Indexer
Proofreaders: Mrs. Ogechi Obi
Foreword: Dr. Victor E. Dike

Print History:
November 2014:   BW Edition

This book is dedicated to my late mother (my guardian angel), Mrs. Ukwunnaya Maria Obi.

- Your memory will never fade!!!

Foreword

I am pleased to write this foreword to the book on social media titled, Visual Facebook for Everyone, by Dr. Marcel C. Obi. I followed the progress of this work from begging and I discussed stages of writing with the author with profound interest. I have known Dr. Marcel C. Obi since our undergraduate years from Philips University, Enid, Oklahoma in the early 1980s to University of Central Oklahoma, Edmond, Oklahoma in late 1980s after which we dispersed to pursue our respective academic dreams in other states and re-joined in California in the early 1990s.

Dr. Obi's book is an important piece of work that cannot fail to attract attention among regular users of social media, and particularly, college students and teachers who are probably more users of social media, as they use it to conduct research, and for learning and teaching. Its appeal will also extend to those who have not seen or used Facebook, as it will take them step-by-step to proficiency. Thus, this book is very relevant, timely and significant in various ways:

Firstly, we are in information age and reigning buzzwords of these days are social media and social network. When people use these terms, they are referring to Facebook, Twitter, LinkedIn, among others. In particular, Facebook is a social media website that people use to interact with one another.

Secondly, directly or indirectly, almost everyone is a part of this Cyber frenzy called social media. A News Anchor cannot conclude his or her evening news without inviting the audience to "Like" him or her on Facebook, or "Follow" him or her on Twitter. Equally, business organizations and public agencies (big and small), have their own slice of the social media pie, by finding most effective and profitable ways of using it to improve their businesses. The evolution of the digital world, vis-a-vis Facebook, has eventually advanced to revolutionize how we interact with one another (as noted earlier) and how it impacts individuals and businesses around the globe in varied ways. More importantly, it has brought the entire globe closer, made the global market place more competitive and in essence created borderless world.

Thirdly, another important aspect of this book is that the author warned us that while it may be inviting to jump into the bandwagon of Facebook, it can be devastating to do so without adequate training or proper knowledge of this very important aspect of the social media. In other words, there is a dark side of the buzzwords! For instance, today we hear about cyber-bully that has often been perpetrated against other people, especially the young adults, which sometimes leads to real life threats. On the lighter side it has created some psychological problems such depression. Extreme consequences can be theft, murder, or suicide. The author, therefore, asked: why then are people rushing to be a part of Facebook if it has been considered to be dangerous along with other social networks? The writer's quick answer is that because its benefits outweigh the disadvantages. For instance, being aware that your teenager is troubled by use of social media can help you intervene before it is too late. Being knowledgeable can help you defend against hackers when they phish your system in an attempt to steal or destroy your data.

Nevertheless, in order to take full advantage of the benefits the social network has to offer, Dr. Marcel C. Obi has laid down detailed instructions, with step-by-step illustrations, on how to use Facebook effectively. This is not very surprising because since I have known him, Dr. Obi has always thoroughly completed any project he has undertaken. One of the interesting parts of the book is how the author dedicates a section to addressing the real life threats promoted by Facebook and other social media, and provides guidance for mitigating cybercrimes. He therefore, states:

> *Security and Privacy threats on Facebook are real. These threats have gone beyond the Internet and computer systems, and have become real life threats. The looming danger generated by a simple mouse click cannot be underestimated; it can go a long way to impact lives. Anyone can become a social media victim of some sort, such as a victim of identity theft, cyber-bully, or sexual abuse, which can occur because hackers got into your electronic system and collected valuable information, or because you gave out such information without realizing the level risks involved. Teenagers can easily become a victim to the pedophile that tricked them into giving out their e-mail address and mobile phone number. As Facebook is growing in popularity, attracting almost a billion audiences worldwide, more and more users are now becoming conscious of these online threats. Unfortunately, only few people know how to protect themselves and their personal information [from the prying eyes of those who don't wish us well].*

The book deserves to be highly commended in that it is topical and well written. Thus, I strongly recommend without reservation every aspect of it to the users of Facebook and other aspects of social media. However, my favorite areas are chapters on security and privacy where the author has addressed the real life danger that might occur if users fail to protect themselves, as they should. More importantly, this book offers step-by-step illustrations on how to customize and enhance your Facebook security and privacy settings, and goes further to provide safety tips to teenagers, parents, educators, and the general public.

Victor E. Dike, Ed.D.
Formerly, Adjunct Professor, School of Engineering and Technology and Media, National University (Sacramento Center), is currently the Founder/CEO, Center for Social Justice and Human Development (CSJHD), a non-governmental organization with its headquarters in Sacramento, California that provides educational and training services to underserved groups. Dr. Dike is the author of several books, including Leadership and Governance: Implication on the Nigerian Economy (with Agatha Ekeh and Dr. Meshack Okpala as co-authors), North Charleston, SC: Create Space (January 10, 2014) and Leadership without a Moral Purpose, North Charleston, SC: Book Surge Publishing (2009). Also, he is the author of numerous peer-review articles, including "Leadership and the Nigerian Economy," SAGE Open, 2014 4: DOI: 10.1177/2158244014523792 and "Planned intervention and organizational development: the role of leadership in change initiatives," African Journal of Science, Technology, Innovation and Development, DOI: 10.1080/20421338.2014.902576. For further information, please see www.csjhd.org or contact him via e-mail: vdike@cwnet.com; dr.victoredike@yahoo.com.

Table of Contents

Chapter 1

Facebook: Introduction and Evolution

An Overview

Facebook is a popular free social network website that is dedicated to bringing people together in an online collaboration. Facebook allows interested users to create an online account, with the privilege to connect with friends and family to find out what is happening in their lives; send a message to other users; and upload photos and videos to the website. Users of Facebook also can keep in touch with one another by sharing the uploaded photos and videos in addition to playing numerous online games, using Facebook applications as desktop or mobile app, and use other valuable information the social network makes available to users. Facebook is not only used for individual entertainment, it is utilized by businesses as well, for marketing products/services, and for sales promotions. It is where you want to be if you are looking for people to socialize with or if you have a business to market online.

Facebook was founded on February 4, 2004, by Mark Zuckerberg with his fellow Harvard University students, Eduardo Saverin, Andrew McCollum, Dustin Moskovitz and Chris Hughes. When Mark Zukerberg and his Harvard classmates first created the original Facebook, it was named *thefacebook.* After a year following the inception, it was renamed Facebook. The initial intent of the new social network was to exclusively serve Harvard students. However, beyond the founder's expectations, it immediately became so popular that many students joined the network within the first 24 hours of the site's launching. More than half the student population would join the social network in less than a month. Seeing the progress, Zukerberg and his classmates extended the social network to colleges in the Boston area and other Ivy League schools (The Ivy League institutions include Brown University, Columbia University, Cornell University, Dartmouth College, Harvard, Princeton, the University of Pennsylvania, and Yale University).

Facebook foundation was inspired by the modern day technologies; and rightfully was conceived at the peak of the Information Age. Requirements of information age include the bid for information that is dynamic and can travel fast at high speed. Facebook passed this test with flying colors and earned an A+ with its instant information delivery that can travel across the globe in a matter of seconds. Consumers of the information age are hungry for information exchange that is fast and can drive innovation. Facebook also showed the company is a viable candidate in the area. Some of the technology companies that were started before Facebook that have similarities in upward trends include Google, Apple, and YouTube, just to name a few. Some of these organizations were started in the garage and somehow found a way to become instant successes. Facebook joined this elite group in a storm and quickly surpassed some.

The instant and rapid growth of Facebook caught the attention of many investors. One of those was Microsoft's CEO, Bill Gates, who was instrumental to the future of Facebook. In 2007, Microsoft invested on Facebook by purchasing a 1.6% of its share for $240 million, giving Facebook a total implied value of around $15 billion. With that, Facebook saw an increase in the number of users which hit 50 million user marks. According to Jenny Lyn Bader, "with Microsoft's acquisition of a stake in Facebook, the site has won a famous new convert to social networking!"

Source: http://bits.blogs.nytimes.com/2007/10/30/bill-gates-has-joined-facebook-he-has-friends/?_php=true&_type=blogs&_r=0

Facebook Evolution

The original Facebook was born in 2004 and named theFacebook. In 2005, the company officially dropped the "the", and theFacebook became *Facebook*, paving the way for 2006 re-design which included larger photo and a font that was more pleasing to the eye than the previous design. By 2006, Facebook was made open to the public and everyone at the age of 13 and older with a valid email address was allowed to create an account. In 2006 also, Facebook added two new features: News Feed which appears on users' homepage and Mini-Feed, which appears in each user's profile page or timeline. News Feed highlights what is happening in your Facebook social circles. It updates a personalized list of news stories throughout the day. Mini-Feed is a new part of the profile that shows all your activities on Facebook. Facebook has had continuous change over the past ten years. Its intuitive structure has continued to help interactions among users all over the world. Users are able to create profiles, upload photos and videos, send messages and keep in touch with friends, family, interest groups, and colleagues. Users use the status feature to inform their friends of their whereabouts and what they are doing. The way these features are implemented helps to make the website unique, and probably it is one of the reasons Facebook is the number one social media site in the world today. Part of the original design included the wall, which is a space on user's profile page that allows friends to post messages for others to see. Other interesting components of Facebook evolution are explained here:

Profile Page or Timeline

According to Facebook, your profile page, which is now called your timeline, is a collection of the photos, stories you may choose to share. Facebook introduced Timeline in 2011 during developers' conference with the founder, Mark Zuckerberg. The Timeline includes an ambitious new interface with a large cover photo and an assortment of posts that tell the story of the user's life since joining Facebook, and depending on how much information the user is willing to disclose, the Timeline featured posts can scroll back through the user's history, including birth. Things you can do on your timeline include: add profile photo and cover photo; edit your basic info; jump to stories from your past; view a log of your Facebook activity, star stories you want to highlight; add life events; update your status; view and add photos; and share your app activity.

Photos

Photos application is one of the most popular applications on Facebook. It enables users to upload albums and unlimited number of photos. When compared to other image hosting services such as Photobucket and Flickr, which have limits to the number of photos that a user is allowed to upload, Facebook's **photos app** surpasses all. Privacy settings for an individual album on photos app can limit access based on a group of users. For example, the privacy of an album can be set so that only the user's friends can see the album, while the privacy of another album can be set so that all Facebook users can see it. Another interesting feature of the Photos Application is the "tag" feature which enables users to label a photo. For instance, if a user recognizes a friend in photo, then the user can tag the friend. This sends a notification to the friend that they have been tagged, and provides them with a link to see the photo. Recently Facebook launched a new feature for photo tagging, enabling users to tag "*brand page*" *photos*, *product, company* or the person's homepage, similar to the way they tag their friends' photos within their personal profile.

Facebook Notes

Facebook Notes Application is a simple word-processing feature for Facebook users. A user can use *Notes app* to publish content that is too long to post on a Wall or a publication that requires formatting to fit a certain purpose. While status updates that you post to your Wall have a limited character length and no HTML formatting capability, *Notes* lets you write full-length posts with formatting, tagging and pictures. If you have ever wished you could integrate blogging with your social networking profile, then Notes application may be just what you need. The Notes feature link appears under your profile picture on the left side of your home page.

Facebook Chat

Facebook *Chat* allows users to communicate with friends in real time. It is similar in functionality to desktop-based instant messenger, or mobile phone-based short message service (sms) texting.

Like

Facebook describes *Like* as a way to "give positive feedback and connect with things you care about", www.facebook.com. Like is a social networking feature, allowing users to express their appreciation of content such as status updates, comments, photos, and advertisements. It is also a social plug-in of the Facebook platform that enables participating Internet websites to display a similar like button. According to Facebook, when you click *Like* on a Facebook Page, in an advertisement, or on content of Facebook, you are making a connection. A story about your like will appear on your timeline and may also appear in your Newsfeed. Your *Like* may be displayed on the Page you are connected to, in advertisements about that Page or in social plugins next to the content you like. You may see updates in your feeds and the feeds of your friends from pages you like.

Voice and Video calling

Facebook has enabled the ability of users to make live voice calls via Facebook Chat, allowing users to chat with others from all over the world. This feature lets the user add voice to the current Facebook Chat as well as leave voice messages on Facebook. Video calling services, which uses Skype as its technology partner was also launched to allow one-to-one calling using a Skype Rest API. This feature makes video conferencing among users possible and easy.

Facebook Subscribe (Follow)

Facebook *Subscribe* allows users to see people's public status updates and posts without the need to add them as a friend. In December 2012, Facebook announced that due to user confusion surrounding *subscribe* function, the subscribe button would be re-labeled *"follow"* button, making it similar to other social networks with similar functions.

Year in Review

Marcel C Obi / Year in Review   Marcel C Obi ... 4 profos

Your year in review is a collection of your biggest moments on Facebook of a specific year, including life events, popular posts you have shared and posts your friends have tagged you in. You can generate your *year-in-review* slideshow for the previous years. To do so, visit this location: https://www.facebook.com/yearinreview. Your friends' year in review can be displayed by visiting: https://www.facebook.com/yearinreview/friends.

App Center

App Center application was launched by Facebook on 7 June 2012. The purpose was to help the users in finding games and other applications with ease, and also to satisfy increasingly mobile audience. Since the App Center launch, Facebook has seen an increase of monthly users and application installations.

Graph Search

Facebook launched Graph Search first in March of 2013. The application allows users to search for people, photos, places, and interests within the Facebook search engine by typing simple words or short sentences. Facebook Graph Search provides custom search results based on your own personal data, including information in the profiles of your friends. Once you start typing a search term, Graph Search attempts to complete the search query automatically, suggesting friends with profile or activity matching your search, your existing connections, Facebook pages, and apps. By choosing from the list, Facebook delivers details of the web search results. In the above graph search example, once the suggestion, *find all places named* "hollywood" was entered in search space, the graph displayed results which included the page shown above that also includes friends that liked the page.

Verified Page

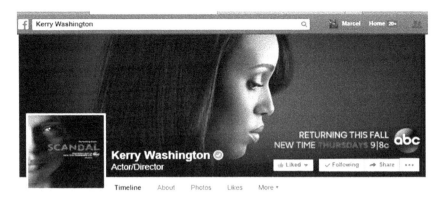

Some well-known public figures and pages with large *followings* are verified by Facebook as having an authentic identity. On a verified page, you will see a blue checkmark next to a verified profile or page name. These profiles and pages may include: celebrities, journalists, government officials, popular brands and businesses. Facebook verifies profiles or pages to make sure they are who they claim to be. Keep in mind that not all authentic profiles and pages are verified and that you cannot request to have your profile or page verified. As shown on the above image, Kerry Washington's page is verified with a checkmark in a blue circle.

Facebook Trending Topics

In January of 2014, Facebook officially announced the launching of a "Trending" section on the sidebar of user homepage. The richer design shows personalized lists of the most news or mentioned words and phrases of the moment with short explanations of why each is trending. On top right corner of the above image of typical newsfeed, notice the *Trending* topics on the right pane. Among tending topics of July 2014 were civil unrest in Ukraine and an outbreak Ebola Fever threatening the whole world.

Facebook Paper

Facebook Paper is an app that helps you explore and share stories from friends and the world around you using desktop or mobile technology. Paper makes storytelling more beautiful with an immersive design and full screen, distraction-free layouts. By introducing paper, Facebook has made it easier for you to craft and share beautiful stories of your own.

Facebook Instagram

Facebook acquired the photo sharing site, the Instagram for one billion dollars in 2012. Zuckerberg commented on the acquisition, calling it "an important milestone for Facebook."

Source:
https://www.facebook.com/bongohive/posts/429159907101475?stream_ref=5

WhatsApp

Facebook acquired WhatsApp in February of 2014, for nineteen billion US Dollars; a purchase that is termed one of the biggest made by the social media giant. WhatsApp is a personal real-time messaging network allowing millions of people around the world to stay connected with their friends and family. It is becoming popular because WhatsApp allows users that signed up to send text, video, and pictures to one another over their existing broadband network, thereby eliminating the need to pay for additional data transmitted as part of the messaging.

Chapter 2
Getting Started With Facebook

Overview

Facebook is easier to use than other social networks in existence today. The sign up process is both intuitive and simple that the initial signup takes about a minute. Account sign up is a requirement since you cannot start communicating with your friends and acquaintances until sign up is complete. During the sign up process, Facebook recommends that you fill out the optional Facebook *profile*, which includes information about your professional and educational background, your likes, hubbies, and so on, in addition to the required fields, in order to enhance your social network experience. Adding photo of yourself and filling the information accurately and completely has benefits and advantages; it will make the site useful to you and those you connect with. Your old college buddies, old acquaintances, and professional contacts cannot find you if your profile information is empty. This is not to say there is no risk to users for entering personal information. Of course, the more information you provide to Facebook or any social media for that matter, the greater the risk that someone may steal or misuse your information. To help you understand how to protect your information, I have devoted a chapter 8 to security and chapter 9 to privacy implications, and discussed methods to protect your personal information so you can have more control over your social network actions. Next step will show you how to sign up for an account, fill out your profile information, and get your personalized Facebook homepage.

Creating Facebook Account

Facebook allows each individual user to create an account for free. Two requirements are needed for an account to be created. (1) You have to be at least 13 years of age. (2) You have to own a valid e-mail address. Once these requirements are met, start up your web browser and browse to www.facebook.com. You can do this with any web browser on your computer, and depending on your platform, your installed browser could be Internet Explorer, Firefox, Safari, or Chrome. Once you succeed in browsing to the site, the landing page or the initial screen looks similar to *Sign Up* image shown on the next page. Description of signup phases and each numbered sign-up box will follow the image.

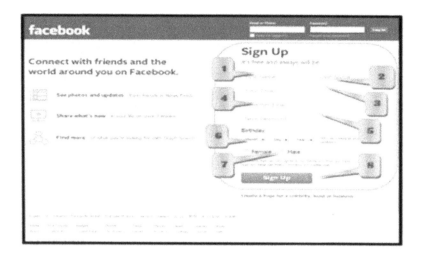

Phase I: Sign Up on Facebook

Facebook requires that you fill-out all the fields in the sign up phase.

1. **First Name**. Facebook expects you to use your real name and avoid aliases. You cannot use special characters, like parentheses or titles with special characters such as Dr., Ms., etc. as part of your first or last name.

2. **Last Name.** Fill-in your last name. Facebook also expects you to use your real last name.

3. **Your Email.** In the **Your Email** field, be sure to type in an active email address as Facebook will be sending you a confirmation notice immediately following your registration. The confirmation email Facebook sends to you contains additional information you need for the completion of the sign up process. If you use incorrect email address, you will not receive the confirmation notice, and therefore, will not be able to complete the sign up. If you are concerned about misuse of your regular email address, you may sign up for additional email address with gmail.com, yahoo.com, or any free email service, and use the new e-mail exclusively for Facebook and other social networks.

4. **Re-enter Email.** In this case, enter the e-mail address you previously entered. It is a way to ensure the e-mail address is error free.

5. **New Password.** Facebook password consists of six-character, or longer, made up of numbers, letters, punctuation, etc. In creating passwords, it is advisable to avoid using part of your name or any information about you that is known by others such as your birthday or city of residence. However, choose a password you can remember and note it down in a secured private location.

6. **Birthday.** Remember, Facebook will not accept your sign up unless your birthday indicates you are 13 or older. Verify your chosen birthday carefully and make sure it is correct and puts you on or above the thirteen-year old age mark or over.

7. **Male/Female (Gender).** Facebook uses the gender information to determine if the user is male or female. At the time of publishing, Facebook had not introduced transgender identifying option, or gay identity.

8. **Sign Up (Button).** After filling all the fields on the sign up form, click on the *sign up* button to complete the sign up. Though your account is created at this stage, it will not be activated until it is confirmed. After you complete the sign up form and submit it, Facebook will send an email to the address you provided in step 3. Click the confirmation link to complete the sign up process. Accept the privacy policy document that appears and move on. If you like, you may read and sign the long legal statements that appear and Facebook will display the three-step process you can use to find people you already know and invite them to become your Facebook friend. Finally upload a photo of yourself as your profile picture so that other people can find and recognize you on Facebook. If you try to sign up with an e-mail address that already

exists on Facebook, be aware that you will be redirected and prompted to login into Facebook instead of proceeding to setup a new account.

Phase II: Optional Steps

Step 1: Find Your Friends

The reason *find your friends* is step 1 on this optional three-step process is to emphasize the importance of finding friends, since the main purpose of Facebook is to give people the opportunity to connect with one another as friends. In this case, your email contact becomes valuable and can be used to send friendship invitation or friend request to those on your email contact. Once you select step 1, find your friends on the **Getting Started** screen, Facebook prompts you to click the name of the email account you use to communicate with most friends, and opens up a dialogue box for you to type the email address. You may choose to bypass this step and Facebook will use the email you signed in with, to generate a mail for recommending friendship request. **Find Friends** button is now displayed against the email account you have chosen. When you click on it, Facebook pops up a box requesting your logon info for the email account. Follow the instructions and Facebook will scan your email account to retrieve email addresses of your contact.

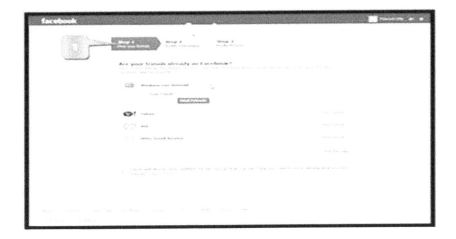

Adding your frequently used email account can make it easy for you to add your friends in a snap. However, it is understandable if users prefer not to give away their email account info to Facebook due to privacy concerns. In this case, you may choose to locate your friends manually by searching, once your account is successfully set up.

Step 2: Profile Information

Facebook *profile* projects user's information that is visible to his or her friends, which includes photos, lists of personal interests, contact information, schools attended, and other personal information. Other information about you that can become part of your profile includes your birthday, your favorite shows, your sexual preferences, and religion. When you first create the account, Facebook automatically creates minimal profile for you based on the information you entered. After that you can opt to enter additional information depending on what you are willing to share on the cyberspace.

People join Facebook and other social network for many different reasons. Your reason for joining the network will play an important role in helping you determine the level of information you are willing to share in your profile. For instance, if your main reason for joining

Facebook is to have the opportunity to checkout other people's profile, or view their photo album, you may want to minimize the information you enter on yours. On the other hand, if you would like potential employers to check you out, or if would like customers to find you, then you should enter extensive information to make it happen. As long as you understand that everything you put on the Internet is subject to misuse and theft, and that Facebook is no different, you will be well guarded to enter your personal information wisely. Also understand that profile building can become a huge undertaking. For this reason, you may enter as much information as you can afford at this time and come back to modify it in the future.

Completing Profile Information

1. Populate the high school field with the name of the high school you attended
2. Populate the college/university field with the name of the college you attended
3. Click the employer field and enter the name of the organization you work for, if you prefer to do that.
4. Current city of residence and hometown fields can be populated respectfully if preferred.

Step 3: Profile Picture

Once you advance to Step 3, you will notice that Facebook has created a place-holder in place of your profile picture, placing a dorky-looking faded image, sometimes referenced as the avatar. Step 3 gives you two options to create your profile photo: **Upload a Photo** or **Take a Photo.**

Option A: Upload a Photo.

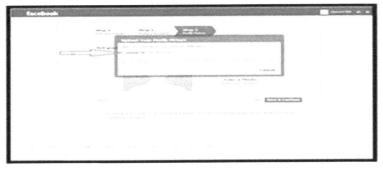

Choose the *Upload a Photo link,* and on the dialogue box that appears, click on *Choose File*, as shown below and browse to the images file you would like to use for your profile picture from your local computer, and click open. Supported formats are .jpg, .png, and .gif. The file will be uploaded and automatically setup as your profile picture which you can change anytime, at will.

Option B: Take a Photo.

Click the *Take a Photo* link option to proceed. But to use the option, you must have a webcam already set up on your computer. Choosing this option will activate your webcam thereby enabling you to have your live photo taken instantly and set up as your profile picture.

When you click on *Take a Photo,* it will automatically communicate with and start up the webcam and your live photo will display on the computer screen, giving you the opportunity to adjust your photo posture. Once you are satisfied with the way it looks, you can proceed to click on the *Set as Profile Picture* button, to have the picture taken and automatically set as your profile picture.

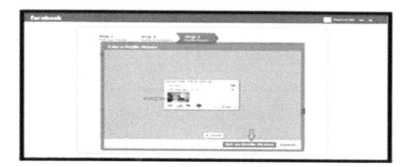

You may now start exploring and using Facebook to the best of your satisfaction as the account setup is now complete.

Chapter 3

Facebook Friends

Friends Overview

Your friends on Facebook social network consist of your acquaintances, past and present; family, teachers, relatives, relatives of spouse, classmates, sports pals, co-workers, friends (past and present), and people from your community focus. Using Facebook tool helps you bring these individuals closer, find new friends, or reconnect with lost ones. The common question people ask sometimes is "why is it important to gain more friends and increase ones social network spectrum on Facebook?" The short answer is, connecting with friends is the whole purpose of Facebook. Facebook gives users the ability to simulate some of the things they do with their friends in real world, such as sharing favorite readings, playing online games, sharing photo albums. It also allows you to share video clips, photos, and so forth, of activities they did not have time to attend. It does not matter to Facebook how you meet people you are friends with. What is important is that both of you have agreed to become friends. In Facebook, two people become friends by way of invitation and acceptance. Usually, the first person initiates an invitation for a friendship, and the second person accepts, or confirms the friendship. And the two people are friends forever, unless one removes or "unfriends" the other. The next section will demonstrate methods of finding a friend and getting connected.

How to Find Friends

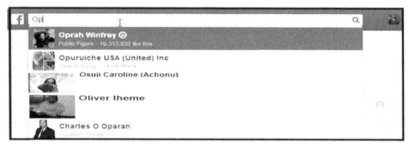

The most direct and easiest way to find a friend on Facebook is to start with friends who are *Facebook users*. You can verify if your friends or acquaintances are on Facebook by typing a name you already know in the search box located on top of any Facebook page. Once you start typing, Facebook will popup names, pages or groups that start with the letter you typed, and as you type additional letters Facebook will continue to narrow the list to fewer names, making it easy for you to find the exact name that matches your search.

Finding People you may Know:

Click the friends icon located on top of your home page to reveal the list of *people you may know*. By clicking on the **People You May Know** button, Facebook reveals people you have mutual friends with and shows their profile photos to make it easy for recognition. You may then click the **Add Friend** button shown on the image, to send a friend's request.

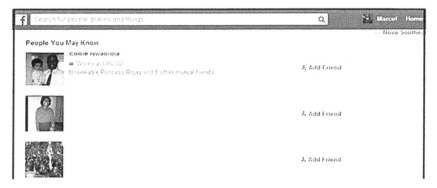

In some instances there may be duplicate names, and that is where the "Face" in Facebook plays an important role. This is because you are likely to recognize one of the profile pictures that displays during your search, to be the friend you are looking for. If so, simply click on the picture to see detailed profile of your potential Facebook friend. You may scroll through the suggested mutual friends, and then send friend's request to the intended friend by clicking the Add Friend symbol as shown in the graphic above.

How to Find Co-workers or Classmates: Step-by-Step

Coworkers or classmates search can produce a list for the category you choose, as long as they have Facebook account. The steps for finding coworkers and classmates are shown below:

Step 1:

Locate the friends' image on the top blue bar. Click on the icon to continue.

Step 2:

Locate and click *Other Tools* at the bottom of the dropdown list which is displayed under "Add Personal Contacts as Friends" page-heading.

Step 3:

Other Tools opens with an option to find classmates and coworkers. Click on the link as shown below to proceed.

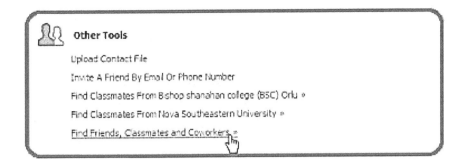

Step 4:

On the find friends from different parts of your life menu, click the checkbox for either school or employer to display classmates or coworkers. Then choose those you would like to add as friends by clicking on the *Add Friend* link

Other Methods to Find Friends

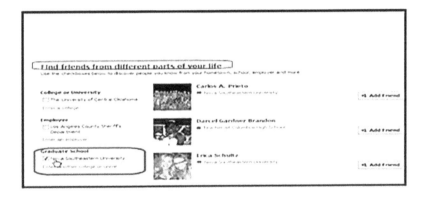

Via Contacts and Webmail

The most popular way of importing friends in mass is by use of contacts. After Facebook imports your contacts, you will have the option to send a friend request to any of your friends that already have a Facebook account (just click Add Friend) or send an invitation to friends who are not on Facebook using their e-mail address.

Invite friends individually

You can also invite your friends individually from the Invite Your

Friends page. Simply enter the email address of anyone you want to invite, add a personal message (optional), and click *Invite Your Friends.*

Note: When you invite friends to join Facebook, Facebook will save a list of those contacts so you can see who you invited and will be able to send reminders. You can always manage list of contacts and control invitations, and reminders.

Finding Friends who are not on Facebook

When you become a loyal Facebook user, it is not unusual to be fervent to connect with some well-known friends, but only to find out they cannot be located on Facebook social network, because they have not signed up. Facebook does not allow you to add people that have not signed-up to Facebook. However, it gives you an easy way to invite non-members.

Who's not on Facebook?

Facebook looks for e-mail addresses linked to Facebook. Anybody in your contacts that is not signed with Facebook will not appear in the search. However, you can still invite them to join Facebook by sending them an e-mail using built in tool, or by using your e-mail system to send the request.

Who is Your Friend on Facebook?

If you like to verify who your friends are on Facebook, **Friend's list** is the most direct way to know who your friends are. Your Facebook friends will appear on your friend's list and your profile page, and vice versa. Facebook makes the relationship between you and your friends visible to anyone with access to your profile. Notice the word *Friends* with a check mark next to the friend's profile picture on the sample friends list that follows.

Automatic Updates to Your Newsfeeds is another one. Your friend's postings will appear on your newsfeeds and your postings will appear on their newsfeeds as well.

Sharing Photos with Friends

Before you can share a photo, you have to upload it to Facebook. If you plan to upload multiple photos, creating Facebook photo album is the right thing to do. Once ready, select the photos you wish to upload and you will be presented with other options.

How to Create Album and Upload Photos: Step-By-Step

To Upload Photo or Video

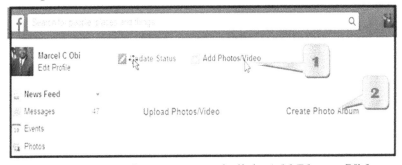

1. Browse to your homepage and click *Add Photos/Video*.

2. Click *Create Photo Album.*

3. This opens up a location on your computer drive so you can select photos to upload to Facebook. The photos display as shown above. Select the ones you like to upload.

4. Click **Open** to start the upload.

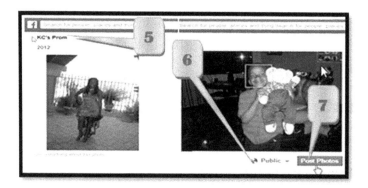

5. **Name the Album and Post Photos.** Once the photos are uploaded, you can give it a title and subtitle.

6. Choose whether to make it visible to the public or select individuals

7. Then, click **Post Photos** to make it accessible to Facebook users. You are done.

Chapter 4

Facebook Messaging and Chatting

Facebook makes message exchange very simple. It may appear difficult at first to use Facebook's great messaging features if you are new to the social network, but once you understand how it works, you will find it easier to use than email systems. In addition, you will discover there are more ways to exchange messages on Facebook than are available with email systems. For instance, with Facebook, you can have live chat with friends; a method that allows you to communicate with one or more friends in real time. You can engage friends in video chat using Skype or similar video communication apps. You may poke your friends sending them an alert that is equivalent to "hi, are you there?" Your understanding of how messaging systems work on Facebook is imperative; as it helps you communicate and exchange messages effectively with your friends, whether they are online or offline.

How Facebook Messaging works

Facebook provides tools to help with user communication or message exchange. The dialogue box used for sending a message to other users' inbox looks like the one used on regular e-mail systems. With the box, you can send a message with text and image content to your Facebook friends and non-friends alike. However, it is recommended that you only send a message to people you know.

How to Send a Message: Step-By-Step

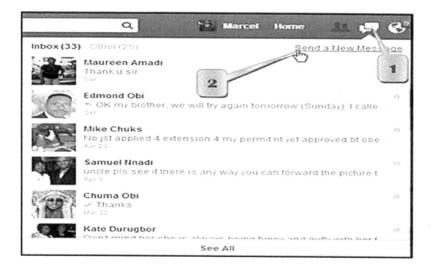

1. Locate and click the speech bubbles on top of your Facebook homepage.
2. Then click the **send a new message** from the displayed page.

Facebook displays the new message box which looks similar to email form, as shown on image that follows on next page.

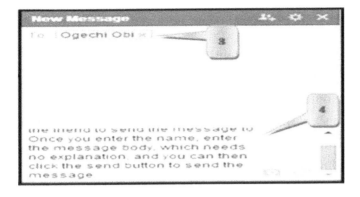

3. On "To:" line, enter the name of the friend to send the message to.
4. Once you enter the name, enter the message body, which needs no explanation,

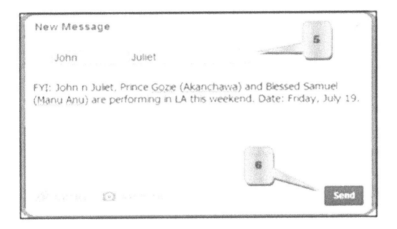

5. You may also send a message to more than one person at a time. However, sending a message to multiple individuals can be a little tricky as Facebook considers some messages sent to several users at a shot as a SPAM. For this reason, Facebook recommends limit of 20 people as the number of one-time recipients. You can enter the names on the To: Line as shown. Alternatively, you can create a friend's list with up to 20 members and just enter the "list" name, and the message will be delivered to each name that is part of the list.

6. You can then click the *send* button to send the message.

How to Chat on Facebook

Facebook makes it easy for you to identify friends that are online so you can chat with them in real time. Chatting, or instant messaging is a popular way to communicate online. However, if you have never chatted before, the concept might seem a little awkward. Not to worry, this lesson will take you step-by-step on how to start and complete a chat session on Facebook.

Starting a Chat Session: Step-By-Step

1. The *Chat Bar* is located at the bottom right of your screen. If chat is turned off, you will notice that the area is grayed out with a display of *Turn on chat ...* Click the "*Turn on chat* to see who's available".

2. The Online Friends window will open and display a list of your Friends who are currently online.

Currently, Facebook identifies a mobile device user with the word "mobile "followed with a green dot. This is a deviation from smart phone image icon previously used to identify mobile users who were online (the image is still used when Facebook cannot quickly determine the network carrier). Desktop computer online user on the other hand is displayed with the word "web" which is also followed with a green dot.

Finding Friends who are Available for Chat

3. Check your Friend's online Chat status.

In early 2014, Facebook changed friends' online status from just green circle symbol to include *web* for those on computer or mobile for those using *mobile* devices. The presence of this indicates the friend is active on Facebook, and is available for chat. The mobile device symbol or simply mobile notation indicates the friend is online via a mobile device. Until recently, a gray Semi-Circle Symbol was used to indicate that a friend is idle on Facebook and cannot respond to a chat. Just recently, Facebook changed it. The spot next to offline friend or friend that is not reachable is represented with a blank white space.

Starting a Chat

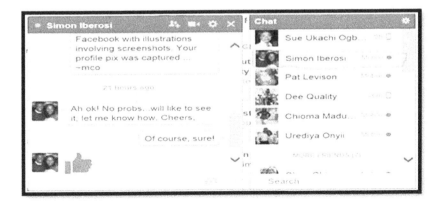

To start a chat session, make sure the intended friend is online by verifying the presence of green web or mobile icon, then click on the Friend's image to open chat window. Begin chatting by typing your message in the message space and by pressing enter on your keyboard to send. Your conversation will be recorded and displayed in the space inside the chat box window. You can open a larger pop out window of Facebook's Chat for a larger view. To do this, click on the chat bar, then Options and select *Pop out Chat*.

Chatting with Multiple Friends

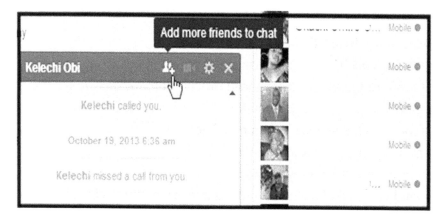

Until recently, Facebook did not allow more than one person in the same *Chat Window*; therefore, the only way to start a chat that involved multiple friends was to create a group. With its new feature, you can now click on the plus (**+**) icon towards the top of your chat window, to include more friends to your chat. You may still create groups for more focused chats. When you create a group and add your friends, you can open a *Chat window* for the group and whoever that is online in the group can respond to your message, and more members can join the chat as they get online.

Hiding Yourself from Chat

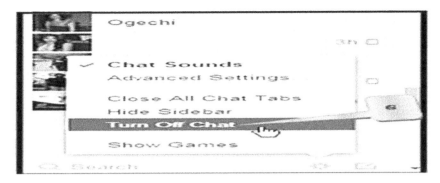

Sometimes you may not be in the mood to chat, or may not want others to know that you are online. If you have a reason to hide your online status while signed on to Facebook, you may do so by turning off your chat. To turn-off your chat, click the Chat tool, then click "Advanced Chat Settings" and select "turn off chart". You may also choose "Advanced Settings" to turn it back on, or to reveal more options which include choice of who to chat with.

6a. When you chose the "Turn Off Chat" from the Options menu, your online status and those of your friends will change in the chat bar to a faded gray background indicating you are offline.

Closing the Chat window

When you are done with the chat, click on the X to close the window.

Deleting Chat Conversations: Step-By-Step

Sometimes you may find chats and messages stored on your profiles to be overwhelming. This is because Facebook automatically saves every single one of your chats and messages. To clear this clutter, you may want to delete your chat history or message history.

To delete one or more messages from a conversation:

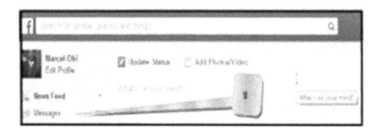

1. Click 🗩 **Messages** on the left side of your homepage

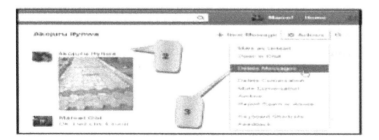

2. Open the conversation you want to delete a message from
3. From the ✱ **Actions** menu, click **Delete Messages...**

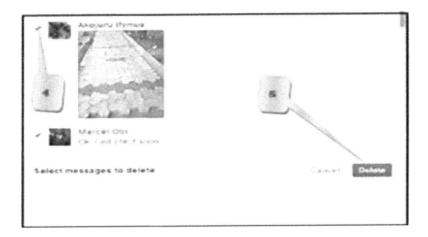

4. Use the checkboxes to select what messages you want to delete
5. Click **Delete.**

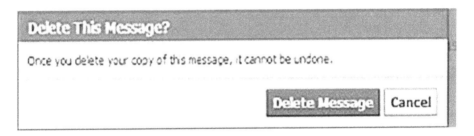

You may also opt to delete an entire conversation by clicking **Delete Conversation** from the ✳ **Actions** menu. Keep in mind, once you delete your copy of this conversation, it cannot be recovered.

To delete part of a conversation, select the messages you want to delete and click Delete Selected. A confirmation window will appear, click Delete Messages.

Note: Deleting a message from your inbox will not delete the message from your friend's inbox.

Video Chat on Facebook

Facebook Video Chatting is relatively new and differs somewhat from regular chatting due to its face-to-face video capability over the Internet. Video calling allows friends to have face to face conversation with each other. To achieve this, you need to complete a quick, one-time setup, after which you are ready to call any friend on Facebook. If you and your friend both have webcams with microphones set up, you'll be able to see and hear each other in real time. If you call a friend who does not have a webcam installed, she will be able to see and hear you, but you will only hear her voice. The time and date of each call you make is listed in your ongoing message history with each friend. The calls themselves are not recorded or saved as part of call records. You will be able to Multi-task during video chats, since it does not disrupt your other Facebook activities.

After you complete the quick, one-time setup, you're ready to make your first call:

1. Visit your friend's timeline and click the **Message ...** button in the top right corner. If you and your friend are already chatting, you can also click the video icon at the top of your chat window.

2. When your friend answers, you may have to wait a moment for your call to connect before the video call begins. If your friend has not set up video calling yet, you will be asked to wait until the setup is complete. It is always a good idea to make sure your webcam and microphone are both up and running.

How to Setup Video Calling: Step-By-Step

1. With Facebook open, navigate to the lower right corner of your

homepage to reveal your friends who are currently online as indicated by the green dots. Choose a Friend to call from the chat window

2. Click the video icon that appears.

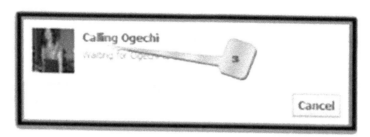

3. The Video Call starts. If the friend's video call has not been setup, Facebook will prompt her to set up video calling.

4. Once the *Install* button is clicked, it will start the application download process.The Facebook Video Call Setup file will begin downloading. At this point, Facebook will provide numbered, step-by-step instructions for setting up video calling. Follow the instructions.

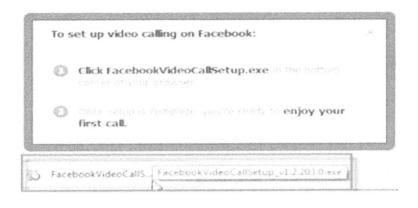

To set up video calling on Facebook: ×

○ Click FacebookVideoCallSetup.exe in the bottom
  corner of your browser.

○ Once setup is complete, you're ready to enjoy your
  first call.

FacebookVideoCallS...   FacebookVideoCallSetup_v1.2.203.0.exe

5. After completing the video setup, the video call will be initiated. Once one person initiates the call, and the other person answers, face-to-face video chat will start.

You are now connected with your friend and you will be able to see and hear each other. To see other options which include full screen view and exit, hover your mouse over the top-right corner of the video. To end the call click the x button that appears at the top right corner when you hover your mouse over the video.

Chapter 5

Facebook Groups and Events

Groups Overview

The purpose of groups is to enable Facebook users organize their family, friends, acquaintances, and co-workers into groups on Facebook. For instance, family members who want to share family photos, former classmates planning class re-union, and support groups that want to share tips and advice, all have good reason to form a group. Being part of a group enables members to share documents posted by other members, post pictures that are only accessible by members of the group, and chat online as a group with members in real time. Facebook Groups app is intuitive that a handful of friends who like to keep in touch with one another on a regular basis can create a group in no time.

Finding and Joining a Group

To become a member of an existing group, you first have to express your interest in the group by locating it and clicking the ***Join Group*** button, which in turn sends a request to the owner of the group, or admin on your behalf. Some of your friends may already own a group or belong to groups owned by others. To reveal existing groups that are visible to you, visit this Facebook location, https://www.facebook.com/groups. Facebook will display a menu that has a list of Groups such as, Friends' Groups, Nearby Groups, Your Groups, and Groups You Admin. Clicking the Friends' Groups menu option will filter groups owned by your friends as shown in the graphic below.

Join a Group: Step-By-Step

1. Search for a group

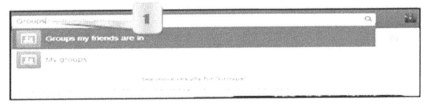

To join a group on Facebook, browse to your home. In the search box, type *Groups* and click *Groups my friends are in.*

2.   Choose a group and click Join

When you find a group and click the *Join* button, it changes to *Request Sent.* For a closed group, admin or owner of the group will approve your request, so that you can get the group privileges. If you change your mind about becoming a group member; you can cancel by clicking the *Cancel Request*, which appears when you click *Join Group.*

Posting to the Group

Joining a group gives you the privilege to:

- Post an update
- Add a photo or video
- Share links
- Ask a question
- Upload a file

Group members get notified when new posts arrive in a group, unless they choose to avoid notifications in their settings. If group privacy is set to Closed or Secret, only group members will be able to see things that get posted in the group.

How to Post and Share in a Group: Step-By-Step

1.   Write Post

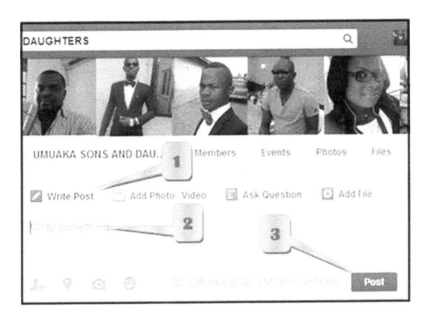

Open a group page and click *Write Post.* You may also click the Add Photo / Video, Ask Question, or Add File.

2. If you wish to write a post, type your update into the field with the display, *Write something.* You may use the buttons displayed under the post to include additional information such as to tag people, include location, upload extra resource information or state what you were doing at the time when the update occurred.

3. Click *Post.* Face*book* sends your post to the group and each member gets an alert.

Create a New Group: Step-By-Step

One of the benefits of creating a group is that it enables group members to keep things private within the group. Group makes it easy to keep in touch with family members who are dispersed throughout the world, project team members, co-workers, and any number of people with a reason to establish a group.

1. To start creating a group, from the left pane of your homepage, click the *Create Group* button.

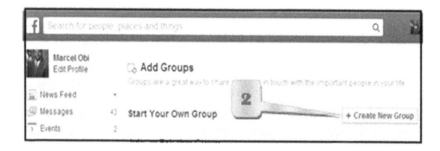

2. Click *Create New Group*. This opens a form to be completed before the new group is created.

Completing New Group Form

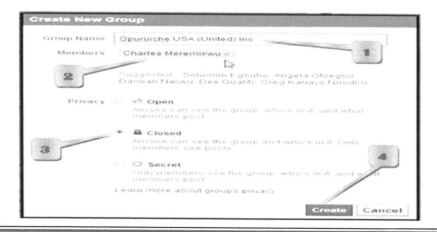

1. Fill out the *Create New Group* online Form that appears. Start by typing the group name.
2. Then, type names of *members* in the member's field. As you type, Facebook pops-up names to choose from which is helpful in speeding up the process.
3. The *privacy* setting is set to *Closed* group by default. It can be adjusted to *Open, or Secret.*
4. When done, click the *Create* button.

Completing the Group Page Settings

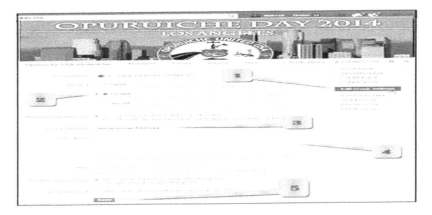

1. Once the page is created, Facebook displays the new group page. Click the gear button, then *Edit Group Settings* to open settings.

2. *Privacy.* This group is created with default settings of *Closed.* This means that each member will be approved before they can use the group and its resources.

3. Create the Group Email Address. Click the *Set Up Group Address* button. Enter the email name and then click the create Email. Facebook checks for the availability of the name you have chosen and creates the mailbox if the name is available.

4. Group Description: Adding group description is optional but it is helpful as an incentive for new members to join. Typing a short description helps members and potential members understand the purpose of the group. To add the group description, on the Group page type a sentence or two on the description field.

5. Click *Save.*

Events Overview

Whenever you are invited to an event by someone, Facebook adds the event to your list of events. Facebook event listings help users find out what is going on around them. The list may include Birthday parties, Graduation Ceremonies, Bridal showers, and even funeral arrangements. On your events page, you can see all events invitation extended to you which Facebook has organized based on the event date but with those happening soonest first.

Types of Event

Facebook Events translate into real-life events. This can raise security, privacy and safety concerns. To help users deal with these privacy issues and safety concerns, Facebook has four event types, namely; *Public Event, Open Invite, Guests and Friends, and Invite Only.*

Until recently, there was only two distinct events, *Public Event* and *Private Event.*

Public Event

This is an open Event allowing any Facebook user to read about it and join the event, if they wish to be part of it. Public Events can be concerts, open soccer events, Festivals, and Fundraising Events. Public events can be identified by presence of an RSVP options of "I'm Attending", "Maybe", and "No"; and with a notation of the word "Public Event" on the Event page.

Open Invite

This type of event is open to all guests and anyone they invite.

Guests and Friends

This type of event allows people invited by the host or guest.

Invite Only

This type only allows people invited by the host.

Creating an Event: Step-By-Step

1. Logon to your homepage and locate *Events* button on the left pane of the page. Click on *Events* to display the events page.

2. On the Events page that appears, click the *+Create Event* button.

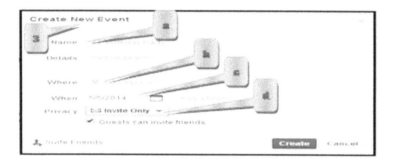

3. The *Create New Event* form displays. Fill out the fields with as much information as you can. Some of the fields that deserve immediate attention are: (a) *Name* – give the event a name that describes it. Choose the name carefully as it helps people find your event quicker. Remember, once the event is created, the name cannot be changed. Therefore, if you change your mind about the name, you have to delete the Event and start all over. (b) *Where* – add location name and/or address, (c) *When* – include the date of event, also click *Add a time* to include event time. (d) *Privacy* – who should be invited to the event. After entering this basic information to create the event, you may come back later to modify it to enter the remaining information.

4. **Edit Event Info** by filling out the form with correct information. Adding complete info helps your friends to find your Event, since Facebook checks at every word entered on the search box to compare with your entry for a possible match.

5. After completing the event creation and adding the event photo, you can start inviting quests. Click the **Invite** button. Total number of people invited will be displayed, with the breakdown between those that are attending and those that responded with a tentative *maybe.*

6. The event is now ready and functional. You may **Write Post,** Add **Photo /Video,** and **Ask Question.**

Chapter 6
Facebook Pages

Facebook users can create pages to promote their personal interests, celebrity image, organizational products, services, or a specific concept. Pages look and behave much like a personal profile, but are designed to attract fans, instead of friends. Fans are people or other pages that choose to "like" your page. A page can gain an unlimited number of fans, while a personal profile can only acquire up to 5,000 friends. Facebook page combines the great features of a personal profile with an interactive nature and amazing features of a public profile and associated marketing scheme. Pages are integrated with Facebook's advertising scheme, allowing owners to easily advertise on Facebook, with the possibility of reaching millions of users that use the social network. This information appears on the page itself, as well as in the personal news feeds of fans. In terms of updating users with statuses, links, events, photos and videos, a page and a personal profile function in the same manner. Pages are suitable for promotional and advertising campaigns.

Page administrator or owner can send status updates to fans. They also have access to tools such as insights and analytics of the page that help them to see their fans base and page activities. Page performance can be enhanced with applications, which can be custom made apps or third-party apps.

How Facebook Pages work

In terms of creating awareness for products or services in the social media era, Facebook pages are on top of the chart. Pages function in the same manner as word of mouth in real world, which has been in use since the beginning of time. Pages are effective in social transmission of information for carrying-out sales propaganda or for running ad campaigns in commerce. Once a user clicks the thumb-up icon on page known as "Like", the user automatically becomes a fan of the page. All updates on the page, will now display on the user's newsfeeds. The information will also be visible to the user's friends, and if the friends like the page also by clicking "Like" button, friends of the friend will also see the page and information posted on it; thereby creating domino-effect, which is good for social advertisement. From now forward, any updates to the page will automatically be delivered to a certain percentage of those that liked the page, also known as fans.

Facebook Page is a key to most social media marketing strategies and can be the central point for most money-making efforts and promotions. It allows users to provide quick updates to the public while also offering full customization and a variety of interactions. Since Facebook page comes with zero cost, it has become safe haven for non-profit organizations, aspiring small business owners, freelancers, and even large businesses that take advantage of its features, to create advertisements without concerns for high cost. Pages give visibility to an organization because they are tailored to meet the organization's needs and customers' demand. Page owners inspire users to like their pages and become fans because the more fans your page has, the more audience you will be able to reach. The audience usually turns into loyal customers for businesses since they are made aware of the products, services, or concepts being offered by the business through the page. Audience reach in today's social media is very essential but not always easy to measure. In order to provide a measure for successful page campaign, some websites are specialized in reporting the popularity of social media sites and comparing them with others. Fanpagelist.com is one example. It measures popularity of Facebook pages based on Total number of Likes. Depicted on the image below is top10 Facebook fan pages for the 1st quarter of 2014.

Top 10 Facebook pages

Source (April 2014):
http://fanpagelist.com/category/top_users/view/list/sort/fans/page1

How to Create a Page on Facebook: Step-By-Step

1. From your Facebook homepage, locate and then Click the *Pages*
   link on the left side pane as shown above.

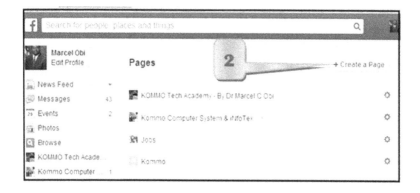

2. From the page that displays, click +*Create a Page* button

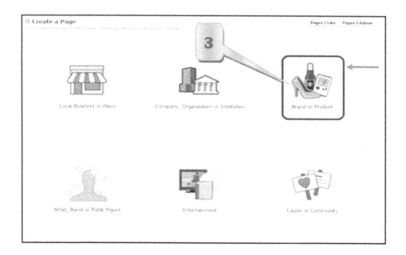

3. Facebook displays *Create a page* screen, with six icons. Each represents a category of pages to choose from. For the purpose of this exercise, I have highlighted the *Brand or Product*. Other categories to choose from are, *Local Business or Place, Company, Organization or Institution, Artist, Brand or Public Figure, Entertainment, and Cause or Community.* The page category you choose to create will depend on the purpose of your page or the message you wish to convey to your fans and the public. Click the *Brand or Product* square icon to move to the next step.

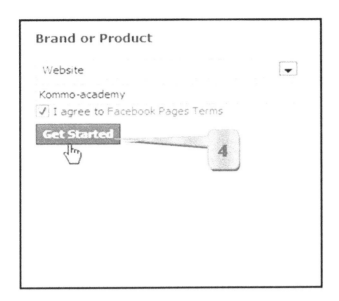

4. Select *Website* from the list of subcategories. Give your page a name. Then, you have to check on *I agree to Facebook Pages Terms* to be able to move forward. Click *Get Started* as shown on page 57, to create the page.

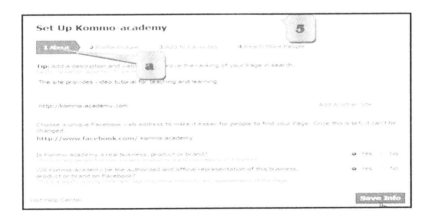

5. Facebook displays a 4-step form to complete the page setup. Each is self explanatory and should be filled-out if necessary, since some fields are optional. The most basic two are *About* and *Profile Picture.*

a. **About:** Type a description of your brand, product, or service into the first text field of number one tab. Be aware that this field takes limited number of characters.

Type a link to your website, Twitter page, or any social media link into the second field. To add more sites, click *Add Another Site*.

In the third field, Facebook asks you to *choose a unique Facebook address to make it easier for people to find your page.* The name you choose becomes a suffix to the original Facebook address, e.g., http://www.facebook.com/kommo-academy. Just remember, once the name is set, it cannot be changed. If you do not have matching information, leave it alone for now, and modify it later when you have the correct information. You only have one chance to modify the default that was automatically added by Facebook.

b. Profile Picture

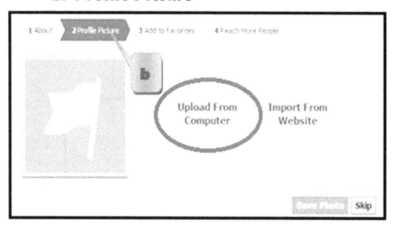

Just like the personal profile setup, page setup allows you to add profile picture and banner to your page. You may upload one from your computer or provide link to an existing picture on the Internet. In this exercise we will upload a profile picture for kommo-academy by clicking *Upload From Computer.*

c. Add to Favorites

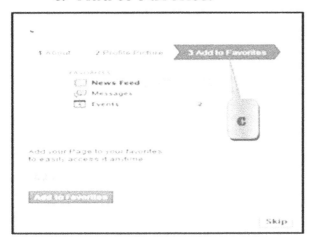

Adding your Page to favorites makes it easily accessible to you at any time, because it will be displayed under favorites at the left pane of your homepage.

d. Reach More People

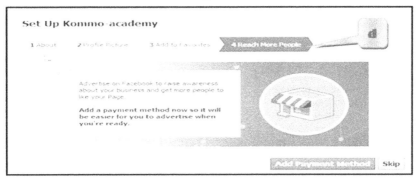

Advertising on Facebook is one of the easy ways to connect with more people. Once you click on *Reach More People,* Facebook displays *Add Payment Method.* The benefit of adding payment method is to make it easy for page owners to advertise whenever they are ready without going through payment setup, each time they do so.

Facebook Page Tab

Facebook page tab is a feature on Facebook that is heavily used. Profit and not-for-profit organizations, and celebrities, use *tabs* to promote their brands or services, or simply to redirect to their *social home.* Page tabs are primarily designed to extend the capability of a page or an application on Facebook. An application on Facebook can enhance the usability of commercial and non-commercial products or services. Applications help you to expand your reach and find more customers with engaging posts on your page. Though applications bring your page to live, they are not easily accessible to your fans without a tab icon, which is a graphic that fans click to get to your website or to your application. Tab icons are popular with Facebook pages. Companies like Gap and Coca Cola have used it effectively to boost fan subscription. Facebook custom tabs could be used to pull in your own custom content alongside the standard tabs such as *Photos* and *Like.* They can also be employed for personal use to share ideas and rich applications. Overall, they allow you to control the content your followers see when they visit your page. Facebook business page layout has gone through changes in recent times. The change means the old way of customizing these tabs has also changed. This section of the book teaches you how to create custom Tabs on the new layout.

Creating Custom Tab Icon: Step-by-Step

Page Tabs are rectangular objects that are lined up under the cover page image (4 tabs are visible at a time). Photos tab is installed by default as the leftmost tabor as the first tab. Facebook does not allow you to move or modify photos tab, therefore, the last photo you add to the photo album, will be displayed by default. The tool to add a tab or modify existing one can be found directly next to the fourth tab image. Follow the 12 simple steps shown below to create a custom page tab and connect it to an app or website.

1. Create Tab Icon Image

To setup your Facebook tab, create an image and have it ready for your new tab. Thumbnail image size 111 x 74; should be descriptive enough to tell people about the website or the app, and what users should expect.

2. Set up a Landing Page

From the search box of your *home*, type *Static*. This will produce a list of *Static HTML: iframe tabs* apps. Click the one with star logo with grey background to proceed.

3. Add an iframe to a page

Click the *Add Static HTML to a Page.* This will prompt you to choose a page to add the tab to.

4. Choose Facebook Page.

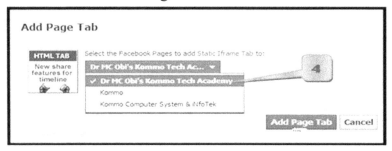

If you have Facebook pages, select one page from your list of pages to install the tab on. If you have no existing pages, Facebook will give you an opportunity to create one. Choose a page and click the *Add Page Tab* button.

5. Authorize the Tab Application

Click the Authorize the Tab. Facebook requires this as a matter of policy so as to be able to contact you in case it finds a problem with one of your pages.

6. The *Welcome* Tab

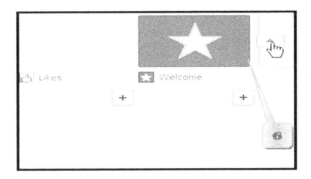

After completing the preliminary as stated above, Facebook creates a *Welcome* tab and inserts it on the page you chose. As the page owner or admin, you will be able to customize the *Welcome* tab, rename and link it to the desired app or page.

7. Add *Custom Tab name* and *change image*

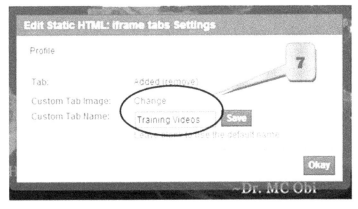

Rename *welcome* to training videos, since the app will pull videos from my YouTube training channel. Replace the start image with the one we designed in step 1.

8. View or Edit Tab

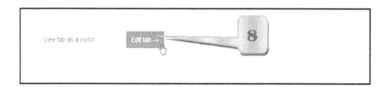

By clicking the **Edit Tab** button, you will be taken to the behind the scenes of a series of applications to choose from that can use the tab.

9. App Templates

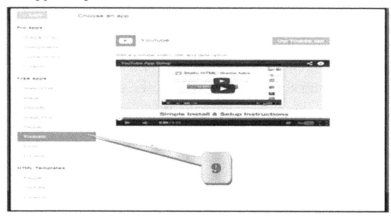

There are three areas of app template to choose from. **Pro apps** offer advanced functionality but may cost extra. **Free apps** require only minor modification of codes, for customization to take effect. A better understanding of html and css is a plus in using apps under **HTML Templates**.

10. Save & Publish

You may now save and publish to make it visible to the audience. Preview tab option gives you the ability to see what the completed app will look like before publishing.

11. Page with tab in place

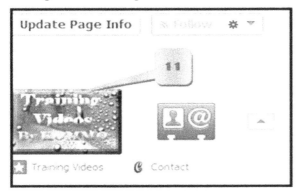

Once tab configuration is completed, the page looks as shown here with all configured tabs in place.

12. End Production View

Concert in Los Angeles Feat Gozie Okeke & Blessed Samuel

The tab is now in full production, and anyone that visits the page will be redirected to the sample video shown above, after clicking the "Training Videos" tab.

Chapter 7

Facebook Applications

Apps Overview

Wikipedia defines Facebook applications as interactive software programs developed to utilize the core technologies of Facebook social network platform. They are tiny programs running inside Facebook that allow users to accomplish certain activities or tasks faster, and in a unique way. They can enhance user experience and make presentation of certain features more appealing and entertaining. Some examples of popular apps are engaging games that can be played inside Facebook, such as Candy Crush Sage, Astro Flux, and Minecraft. You can use apps to share music with friends, share photos, watch movies, read books, send birthday greetings to friends, engage on phone teleconference, and video conference. Applications are important to social media marketing, which is why some of the companies, such as Facebook encourage you to build social apps on their platform for use with web and mobile devices. Facebook in particular offers some incentives to people who develop good applications.

Facebook believes that its appeal to developers would lead to long term benefits for the company, its customers, and the developers. In order to promote third-party developers base, Facebook opened up its developers' platform in May 2007, to allow third-party developers to build applications and widgets that, once approved, could be distributed through the Facebook community. In May 2008, its engineers announced Facebook Connect, a cross-site initiative that allows users to publish interactions on third-party partner sites in their Facebook newsfeed. In March 2012, Facebook implemented the App Center, an online mobile store which markets applications that connect to Facebook. The store is now available to web users, iPhone, Android, and other mobile platforms.

Popular Facebook Apps for Fan Engagement

It is obvious that many eager developers have answered the call to partner with Facebook to develop cool apps for use with the web and mobile devices. Apps for personal fun and serious business are now available and can be found at https://www.facebook.com/appcenter. Users who know how to code the html, php, etc., can develop their own custom apps. You may also hire a programmer to build custom apps for you if it is important to your personal or business life.

Following are examples of third-party apps on Facebook that are available to users:

Phixr Photo Editor

Source: https://www.facebook.com/phixr

According to the app developers, Phixr is a photo editor that lives inside your web browser. It has hundreds of exciting filters and effects for making your favorite shot a piece of pure art. If you are tired of the standard filters everybody uses, Phixr is the place to go. Its sheer features will make your photo easily stick out of the masses. Phixr has the basic tools for cutting, rotating and mirroring your picture. You can fix red eyes, do a tilt-shift, apply all sorts of color effects, add text, gradients, icons, borders, backgrounds and picture frames, apply geo-tags, and do many other things. On Facebook, you can edit the photos from your albums, or those of your friends' and upload your finished work into your Facebook album.

Astro Flux

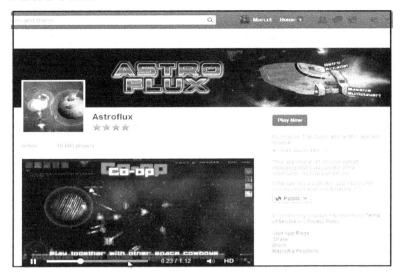

Source: https://www.facebook.com/Astroflux

Astro Flux app is space shooter game with numerous weapon capabilities. It engages you in exploration of the galaxy while you collect space junk to gain resources for new technologies. Facebook users have the privilege of playing this game on the web or via their mobile app.

Booshaka is an application that will highlight the fans who are participating on your page more often. When you install the application, a custom tab called Top Fans is added to your page. Fans get the most points for posting to your wall and they also receive points for comments and likes. You can view the stats of each fan listed to see how they have participated. The app gives a complete history of the fan's activity on your page. Booshaka believes that every consumer is unique, and therefore, segments your audience so you can deliver the right message to the right consumer.

Minecraft

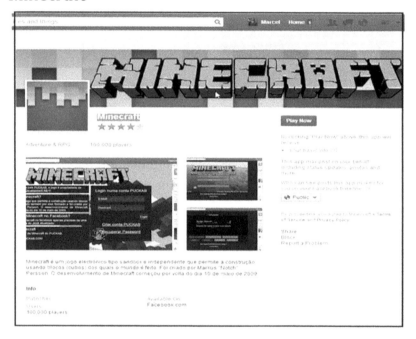

Minecraft is a sandbox indie game. The creative and building aspects of Minecraft allow players to build constructions out of textured cubes in a 3D procedurally generated world. Survival requires players to acquire resources and maintain their health, hunger, and creativity.

YouTube Channel

YouTube channel is an ideal app to integrate it into your Facebook page so people can easily access your videos. This YouTube for Pages is designed by Involver. It is easy to install, the layout is nice and it offers easy sharing. Your most recent video is automatically displayed as the largest. The application will not automatically post your newest video to the wall, but you can easily post it with just two clicks.

Livestream

Livestream is a great way to bring live video events to your Facebook page. The chat feature can make it more interactive with the audience. Events can be live or recorded for later viewing.

Foursquare

Foursquare is used by over 5 million Facebook users and it helps you and your friends make the most of where you are, including:

Share and save your experiences wherever you go

Get personalized recommendations and deals which are based on where you have been and your friends' social behaviors.

Search for anything from free Wi-Fi to best coffee shop or browse popular categories.

Discover insider tips and lists from local experts, brands, and celebrities.

Facebook Custom Applications

Using pre-built apps as shown above is best fitted for personal use. However, if you own a business, or have the need to promote a product or service, building an app on Facebook gives you the opportunity to deeply integrate into the core Facebook experience. Your app can integrate with many aspects of Facebook.com, including the News Feed and Notifications. All of the core Facebook Platform technologies, such as Social Plugins, the Graph API and Platform Dialogs are available to custom Apps on Facebook.

How to Create a Custom Application: Step-by-Step

1. From your Facebook homepage, locate the DEVELOPER menu on the left pane, hover your mouse over the area to reveal <u>More</u> dropdown menu and click. The developers' page will display.

2. You will be redirected to: https://developers.facebook.com/apps and all your existing apps will be listed, if any. To start creating apps, one option is to click the dropdown arrow next to the Apps menu, or go to step 3.

3. Click the *Create New App* as shown on the above graphic.

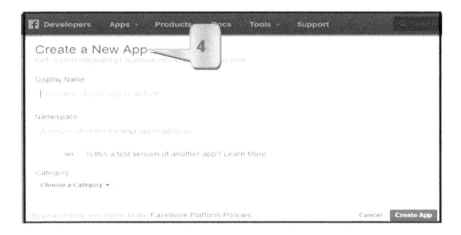

4. The *Create a New App* form displays as shown above.

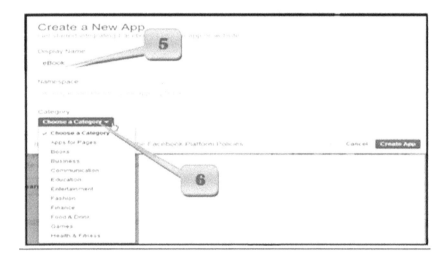

5. Enter your app name on the *Display Name* field
6. Click Choose a Category from category menu.

There are many categories of apps that can be added to Facebook.
Examples include, Apps for Pages, Books, Business, Communication,
Education, Entertainment, Fashion, Games, etc.

7. Under the *Security Check*, fill in **Text in the box** exactly as it appears above. This assures Facebook the form is being completed by someone other than some robots or malicious software program.

8. Once you enter the correct security info, the Dashboard page displays. Click settings to move to the next option; then click *Add Platform*.

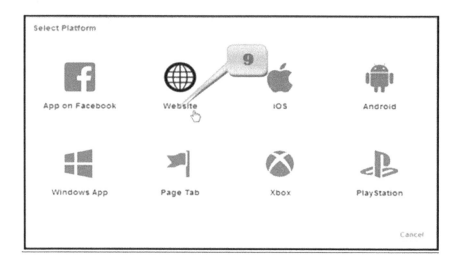

9. Once you select platform page, click Website. You will enter the URL of the website. On your website, you will enter App ID and App Secret sent to your email by Facebook to complete the setup.

How Custom Apps are used on Facebook

Apps on Facebook are web apps that are loaded in the context of Facebook in what is referred to as a Canvas Page. You can build your app using any language or tool chain that supports web programming, such as PHP, Python, Java or C#. When a user makes an App request, it is loaded into a Canvas Page. A Canvas Page is a placeholder or a blank page within Facebook on which to run your app. You populate the Canvas Page by providing a Canvas URL that contains the HTML, JavaScript and CSS that make up your app. When a user requests the Canvas Page, the Canvas URL will be loaded within an iframe on that page. This results in your app being displayed within the standard Facebook space.

Chapter 8

Facebook Security

Security Overview

Security and Privacy threats on Facebook are real. These threats have gone beyond the Internet and computer systems, and have become real life threats. The looming danger spawned by a simple mouse click cannot be underestimated; the looming danger generated by a simple mouse click cannot be underestimated; it can go a long way to impact lives. Anyone can become a victim of Internet fraud of some sort, such as a victim of identity theft, cyber-bully, or sex abuse, which can occur because your electronic systems have become vulnerable to hacker attack leading to your valuable information being compromised, or because you gave out such information without realizing the level of risks involved. Teenagers can easily become victims to the pedophile that tricked them into giving out their e-mail addresses or mobile phone numbers.

As you use Facebook, one thing to bear in mind is that Facebook as social network, has same vulnerabilities just as any Internet organization. This means your information can be intercepted by hackers while logged on to Facebook. Hackers are a huge threat to your sensitive information as they phish for ways to break into accounts or devices that hold your valuable information. Users sometimes relegate their information to threats, either by accident, or lack of knowledge.

As Facebook is growing in popularity, attracting over a billion audiences worldwide, more and more users are becoming conscious of these online threats. Some fear that their Facebook account may even be taken-over by the hacker which may lead to lives being impacted. Regrettably, these concerns are legitimate. Facebook makes your information and posts available to the public by default, but it also empowers you to control your own security and privacy settings according to your preferences. As a user, you need to know the steps to change your Facebook security settings. This is easy as you don't have to be a technology expert to change the security settings. Since you have this book, the problem is almost solved. You are close to getting the rest of mind you deserve because this book is written with you in mind. This section of the book offers step-by-step illustrations on how to customize and enhance your Facebook security settings. It goes further to provide safety tips to the teenager, the parent, and the teacher. You will be introduced to the simple step by step method to modify your Facebook security settings, so that you can take advantage of its rich features.

Providing a secure Internet environment where you can safely access personal account information is very important. Facebook security team is doing a good job in issuing users accounts with default secured settings. However, it is important to enhance those settings according to your personal preferences. The best way to enhance the security settings of your Facebook account is by adjusting the settings for browsing, login, apps usage, e-mail and password. Making sure your Facebook URL starts with https is a way to grantee the data you exchange with others is encrypted on the wire, and therefore are secured. The encryption is important and worth practicing as it makes it difficult for people to access your Facebook information without your permission. Other methods of improving your security include setting up a notification to inform you when your account has been accessed, as well as allowing only approved computers and devices to login to your Facebook account. This section will discuss step-by-step approach that will enable you to enhance these security settings so that you can enjoy your Facebook experience in the most secure manner.

Facebook Security Settings: Step-By-Step

1.   To get started with security settings, login into your Facebook account. From your homepage, locate the dropdown menu icon at the top right corner, and click on it.

2.   On the displayed menu, Click *Settings*.

3. Click Security – *"Security Settings"* opens with many sub-sections to setup. First on the list is *Login Notification.*

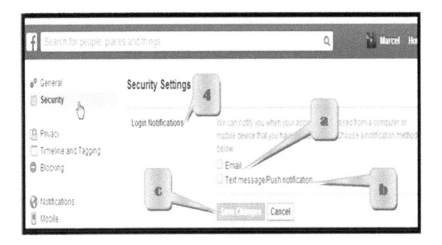

4. Login Notifications

To receive an alert when your Facebook Account is accessed from a computer or a device you have not used before, you need to turn on notifications. Notifications can be sent to you via e-mail, by text, or push notifications to your mobile phone. These notifications can help to alert you of a potential security violation, especially if you maintain the practice of using one computer or a mobile device only to logon to your Facebook account.

Click *Login Notifications.* Facebook uses this to notify you when your account is accessed from another computer or mobile device other than the one you regularly use.

a. Put a checkmark on email as your notification method, if you prefer.

b. If you decide to be notified by text, choose *Text message Push notification*.

c. Click *Save Changes* to Save your changes.

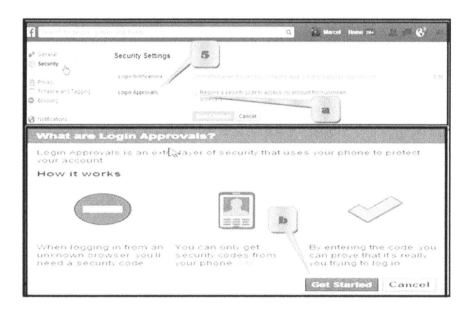

5. Login Approvals

If *Login approvals* is enabled, Facebook sends a security code to your cellular phone when you or someone attempts to login to Facebook from unauthorized computer or device. Unauthorized computer usually is a computer you have not used in the past to logon to Facebook. Entering the code certifies that account is truly yours, i.e., you are not hacking into someone else's.

Click *Login Approvals* to start editing login approvals section

a. Check the ***Require a security code to access my account from unknown browsers*** checkbox

b. Click ***Get Started***

6.   App Passwords

"***App passwords***" is one-time password you can use to log in to your apps and help keep your Facebook password safe. If you have login approvals turned on, you won't have to wait to receive a code when you use app passwords. Instead, you can skip login approvals and log in immediately.

Click ***App passwords***

a. Click ***Generate app password.*** Type in the name of the App and click Generate Password. Go to your app and use that password to log in.

7.   Trusted Contacts

Trusted contacts are friends that can securely help you if you ever have trouble accessing your account. Trusted contacts are close friends that you can call for help if you ever have trouble accessing your account.

Under *Security Settings*, click the *Trusted Contacts* tab.

a. Click *Choose Trusted Contacts* Link

As a rule of thumb, choose 3 to 5 friends that you can call for help if there is ever a problem with your account. Then, Click the *Confirm* button to trusted contacts.

8.   Trusted Browsers

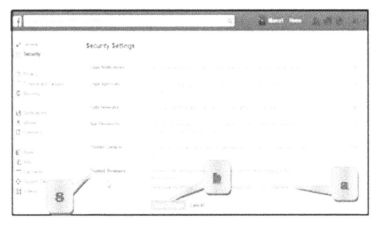

In *Trusted Browsers* section, all devices that have been authorized to use Facebook account are displayed. Devices will only be displayed here if you are already using Login Approvals. Each time you login to Facebook from an unknown device and use a code sent to your mobile phone to authorize the device, the list is populated with the new device. You can remove a device when it is no longer needed or lost, by selecting and clicking "Remove".

Under *Security Settings*, locate and click the *Trusted Browsers* tab.

    a.   You can remove an unwanted device by clicking the *Remove* button, against the device.

    b.   Click the *Save Changes.*

This will save all the changes you made.

9.   Where You're Logged In (Active Sessions)

The active session in *Security Settings* shows where and when your Facebook account has recently been accessed. More often, this shows your account login status. You should review this periodically, if you are curious and concerned that someone else may have been accessing your account. The screen also shows the active sessions, and if you notice suspicious logon to your account, you have the option and capability to end the suspicious session.

Find and click the *Where You're Logged In* section to expand its settings.

a. Click *End all activity* to end all logins to your account

b. Click *End activity* to end a specific login to your account. Once you click *End activity,* the ended activity will be removed from the list.

Chapter 9
Facebook Privacy

Facebook Privacy Settings

Facebook has grown in popularity since its inception in 2004, attracting over a billion users worldwide. With the growth of Facebook, also comes growing concerns for user privacy. Because of these concerns, it is no longer easy to enjoy all the advantages the social network has to offer without thinking about minimizing the risks associated with privacy issues. Facebook is conscious of these risks and has delivered the website with preconfigured privacy settings. While the default settings may be good enough for some users, it is not nearly enough for users who are privacy conscious.

Facebook gives you a greater control of your privacy settings. It lets you control who can see information about you; the photos, videos, and other updates you post. It also lets you set up a method to connect with friends, as well as determine how much of your information is shared with applications, games, and websites via Facebook. Understanding the privacy problems, which are taught in this book, will empower you to preserve your online privacy. For instance, you should understand that Facebook embeds your information such your likes, your political interest, religion, city you live in, your relationships and social habit to the information you share with others. If you become knowledgeable of the looming threats that are associated with personal information you share, you will be able to make the right decision whenever you share your information. This knowledge will help you reduce the risks while at the same time enjoy the benefits of this great social media website.

Facebook Privacy Threats

To avoid privacy threats, do the following:

- **Keep Your Private or Sensitive Information Private**
  Before posting any information on Facebook and making it public, think about it to determine if it belongs there. Identity thieves can only steal information that is online or on the Internet. Information like your social security is too costly for compromise, therefore, be careful if you have to use it for an online transaction, at the least, make sure it is a secure and encrypted online transaction.

- **Reporting Suspicious Activity**

  With a billion users, Facebook encourages its users to report any content that violates their Community Standards. These reports enable their team of review professionals to quickly and effectively remove abusive content from Facebook. Today, Facebook is excited to announce initial testing of a feature that allows you to see what happens after you click *Report*. Facebook made this move because they have consistently received feedback that once people report something to them, they did not know where it went or whether it was handled. This new feature alerts users when a decision has been made about the report they made. Once a report is addressed by Facebook's User Operations team, the person who made the report will receive a notification that her report has been reviewed or she can go directly to the Support Dashboard in her account settings. With this reporting enhancement, **victim of** Cyber-Bully or online harassment; or witnesses to the crime being committed on other users, are encouraged to report the activity to Facebook. According to Facebook, such crimes are sometimes perpetrated by someone from their past, or by a total stranger. Facebook further states it is providing information to help users as follows:

> *At Facebook we maintain a robust infrastructure that empowers our more than 900 million person community to help us enforce our policies by using the report links found throughout the site. While it is unlikely that you will have any problems with content on the site, it might not always be clear what happens once you do decide to click "Report." Today, we are excited to publish a guide that will give the people who use Facebook more insight into our reporting process.*

> *There are dedicated teams throughout Facebook working 24 hours a day, seven days a week to handle the reports made to Facebook. Hundreds of Facebook employees are in offices throughout the world to ensure that a team of Facebookers are handling reports at all times. For instance, when the User Operations team in Menlo Park is finishing up for the day, their counterparts in Hyderabad are beginning their work keeping our site and users safe ... no matter where they are.*

The sample reporting guide is provided at this link:
https://www.facebook.com/notes/facebook-safety/what-happens-after-you-click-report/432670926753695

- **Protect Your Login Information**

  Make every effort to prevent someone other than yourself to login to your Facebook account. It does not matter if the individual is your family member or a co-worker. One way to achieve this is by making sure the "Keep me logged-in" checkbox is unchecked at logon, and be sure to logout completely at the end of each Facebook session, especially if you use public computer or a device that is shared.

As a final thought, the important thing to remember is that the same information embedded in the photo you share, your likes, your comments and statuses can become a threat if it falls into the hands of a total stranger.

Keeping Your Facebook Information Private

It is unfortunate that many users simply do not pay attention to their privacy settings on Facebook. This careless behavior on the part of the user has resulted in a notable number of privacy issues on Facebook, which range from embarrassing photos being revealed, the user being harassed, to people being fired from their job for making negative remarks about their workplace. Proper controls of privacy settings could keep information private to help you avoid some of these problems, though it is understandable that securing your information and keeping it private after it is uploaded to Facebook can be an arduous task. But, do not worry. The good news is, since you have this book, your job is done. Just follow the clear directions and steps that are provided in the next session titled, "Changing Facebook Privacy Settings" which shows you how Facebook puts much of the power into your hands, and allows you to use its easy to follow tools to achieve this goal. You will discover that Facebook offers a range of privacy options to its members. And that a user can make all his communications visible to everyone, block specific ones or keep all his communications entirely private. Users can choose what not to put in their newsfeed and determine exactly who can see their posts, all from the comfort of the privacy settings tools.

Tips - Some privacy highlights

- By default, the information you share on Facebook is publicly visible. This is good reason to customize your privacy settings
- Some information from your profile, such as your name, profile picture, and gender will always be considered public, no matter which privacy settings you apply. This means, they will be visible to the public

Changing Facebook Privacy Settings

Facebook Privacy is focused on empowering you to control the privacy settings of your Facebook account. The empowerment features will help you determine and choose who to share your information with. When you sign up with Facebook, your privacy settings are set to the default, which means your information is made available to the Public. It also means that everyone on Facebook and anyone who searches for your name on the web can see your personal information. Therefore, it is recommended that you change your privacy settings on Facebook because customization of privacy settings allows you to control who can see what you have posted. While it cannot completely eliminate privacy threats, it will reduce the chance of your information falling into the wrong hands. The knowledge you gain by reading this book will help you determine what information you can control, and how Facebook shares your information across the web using the Facebook Platform. The steps for customizing your privacy settings are illustrated below.

Customizing Privacy Settings: Step-By-Step

1. From your Facebook homepage, click the pull-down menu symbol (inverted triangle) on the top right.

2. On the list that appears, select and click *Settings.*

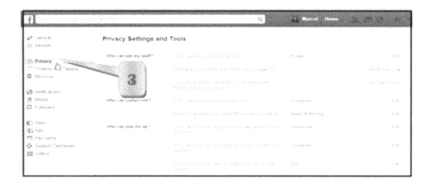

3. Click *Privacy* tab to reveal *Privacy Settings and Tools* setup options.

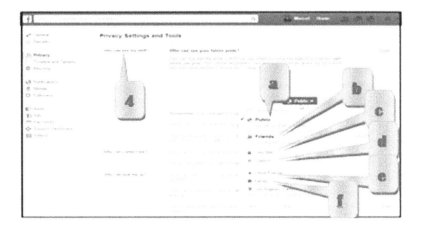

4. ***Who can see my stuff?*** This section empowers you to control how things you post can be shared and it has many options to choose from, including:

   a. Public
   b. Friends
   c. Only Me
   d. Custom
   e. Close Friends
   f. Family

In addition to configuring the above settings in advance, you can also manage the privacy of things you share by using the audience selector right where you post. This control remembers your selection so future posts will be shared with the same audience unless you change it.

5. *Who can contact me?*

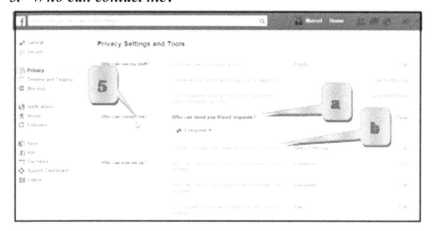

a. ***Who can send a friend request?*** The default is ***everyone.*** Anyone with Facebook account can send you friend request. You may leave this unchanged, especially if you are new and want to get as many friends as possible. The second option is ***Friends of friends,*** which only allows friends of your friends to send friend request to you.

b. ***Whose messages do I want filtered into my Inbox? Basic filtering*** is recommended and it allows your friends and people you may know to send a message to your inbox. With ***Strict filtering*** you can see message from your friends and people you like to hear from.

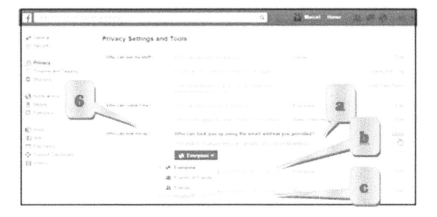

6. ***Who can look me up?*** There are three areas you use to enhance privacy settings of your Facebook account under who can look me up. These include:

    *a. **Who can look you up using the email address you provided?***

    *b. **Who can look you up using the phone number you provided?***

    *c. **Do you want other search engines to link to your timeline?***

How you respond to the above settings will depend on your personal interest and affiliations. The important thing is that Facebook gives you the ability to control who you want to be part of your information dissemination.

Privacy for Minors on Facebook

The first rule to understand is that Facebook does not allow children under the age of 13 to establish an account. It however offers extra privacy protection for minors under the age of 18 which is limited. Just like adults, minors' information will show up in public search results, and anyone can view their most basic information, such as name and profile picture. Children are hit the hardest when it comes to Internet crime, due to their unsuspecting nature, and high level of trust they hold on others. There have been cases where children are cyber-bullied, and the end results of some of the cases are not pleasant. Since most children do not have a good perception of privacy implications, it is therefore incumbent upon parents or guardians to emphasize the importance or help them set up privacy controls. If this is not done, their personal information, including contact information, photos and updates, can be viewed by their Friends and Friends of Friends, which may interpret to a total stranger down the line. Help your children to set their privacy settings high and inform them to refrain from adding thousands of friends they don't even know. Having a very good control of your child's activities on Facebook and Social Media as whole will not only protect them against hacker, malware and virus, it will help save lives.

Facebook Safety Tips

Facebook folks believe safety should be part of conversation and a shared responsibility among all people and that is why they provide the information, tools and resources you will need to make it work. There is responsibility for everyone, parents, teachers, teens and the law enforcement.

Tips for Parents

1. It can be tough to keep up with technology. Don't be afraid to ask your kids to explain it to you.
2. If you're not already on Facebook, consider joining. That way you'll understand what it's all about!
3. Create a Facebook group for your family so you will have a private space to share photos and keep in touch.
4. Teach your teens the online safety basics so they can keep their Facebook timeline (and other online accounts) private and safe.
5. Talk about technology safety just like you talk about safety while driving and playing sports.

Help Your Teens Play It Safe

In the past, teenagers spent much of their free time talking to friends on the phone. Today, the mode of communication has changed. They just have more ways to communicate which include Facebook chats, tweeting, photo and video exchange, and live video conferencing. Today's teens have grown up with the internet, cell phones and text messaging. Most don't distinguish between being online or off. New technology has always been a part of their lives. So, instead of writing it off as trivial or a waste of time, thereby criticizing a big part of their social interaction, you need to learn the ropes to be able to help them. You don't have to become technology expert to help your children.

What's My Teen Doing on Facebook?

Just like adults, teens use Facebook to connect with friends—through chat, personal messages and sharing photos, videos, links and other kinds of information. They use Facebook to announce achievements, wish each other a happy birthday and plan social events - like going to a movie or meeting at a friend's house.

Who Can See My Teen's Timeline?

The only people who can see what teens post are their Facebook friends, friends of friends, and networks they belong to such as (the school they attend, etc). Facebook maintains added protections and security settings for teens (age 13-17) that ensure their timelines and posts don't show up in public search results. Similarly, if teens share their location through Places, only their Facebook friends can see it. Encourage your kids to utilize the *View As* tool on the top right side on their timelines. They can see what their timeline looks like to the public. To preview how their timeline appears to a specific person, type the name of the person into the open field and press enter.

*View As...*The most direct way to get here is to open your timeline page, click on the three dots to reveal a menu which includes *View As...*shown below on the image.

Click on the *View As...* to display the options shown below. The first choice will show you what members of the public will see, once they visit your timeline. *View as Specific Person* will display and show what a particular friend sees.

Start a Conversation with Your Teen

Parents do not need to be social media experts in order to ask questions and begin an ongoing dialog with teens. Have conversations about safety and technology early and often, in the same way that you talk to your kids about being safe at school, in the car, riding public transportation, or on sports field. Learn some *Facebook Lingo* such as *timeline, profile, friends, friends of friends, like, poke, wall, inbox;* to help you with the conversation. For instance, *Friends* are people you connect and share information with on Facebook. Friends of friends are other friends they are connected with that are not yet your Facebook friends.

Reciprocity of Online Respect

Some parents may be skeptical about becoming their children's friends, but is perfectly ok to do so. If you become your child's friend on Facebook, try to respect the same boundaries that separate you offline. Your relationship should dictate how you interact with your teenager on Facebook. It is all about balancing your teen's growing independence and the need for privacy with your safety concerns. It is also important to talk about the Golden Rule: remind them about treating others the way they want to be treated. Make sure your teens know where to go for support if someone ever harasses them. Help them understand how to make responsible and safe choices about what they post—because anything they put online can be misinterpreted or taken out of context.

Tips for Teachers

1. Study your school's policy about using social media in the classroom, and comply.
2. Use public pages for your classes to post homework assignments and other updates.
3. Use groups to control membership and facilitate discussion.
4. Be a role model of a good online citizen.
5. Report inappropriate content to Facebook.

Teaching Digital Kids

Today's teenagers are growing up in a digital world. Teachers can play an important role in keeping teens safe, inside and outside of the classroom, knowing that technology is all around us, and that your students will continue using cell phones and social media, even when they are in school. It is true that most adults are not as active with social media and new technologies as the younger generation, teens are still looking to them for examples of how to be good citizens—online and offline. This is the main reason Facebook encourages educators to engage with students online and follow closely the guidelines of their different schools and district's varying policies about the use of social media in the classroom.

Facebook in Classrooms

You can use Facebook as a communications hub for you and your students. You can achieve this by creating a public page or smaller closed group for your classes to keep parents informed, distribute homework or permission slips, and share photos or videos from classroom activities or field trips. Anyone can like a page on Facebook, and students who do will see updates in their News Feed. *Facebook Groups*, on the other hand, allows you to limit membership to only those you approve. You can also email all the members of a group. Maintaining a page or a group is also a great way to establish a presence as a teacher without blurring the line between your personal and professional lives. You can interact with parents, students and colleagues via your page or group.

Tips for Teens

1. Don't share your password with anyone.
2. Only accept friend requests from people you know.
3. Don't post anything you wouldn't want your parents, teachers, or employer to see.
4. Be authentic. The real you is better than anything you might pretend to be.
5. Learn about privacy settings, and review them often.

Be Yourself on Facebook

How you present yourself on Facebook says a lot about who you are— just like what you say and do at school or with your friends. It is important to represent yourself as the kind of person you are. As a smart person, use good judgment whenever you are online. Facebook is a community where people use their real names and identities, so they are accountable for their actions. To be part of this great community, try to be honest and play by the rule.

Think Before You Post

Be aware that any information you post, whether it is in form of comment, note, or video chat could be copied, pasted, and distributed in ways that you did not intend. Before you click the post button, ask yourself if you would be embarrassed to share the content with your parents, teachers, or future employer. Sometimes, it is easy to get caught up in the moment and write or do something that may seem hilarious at the time. But remember, what you say can hurt someone, or even worse, it can come back to haunt you.

Chapter 10
Facebook Marketing Concepts

Use of social media to promote products and services is on the rise as businesses try to embrace the new marketing concept. Since social media allows business owners to build relationships with their customers, many organizations are now using Facebook for marketing campaigns due to its social media advantage over others. One of the advantages is the cost to advertise on Facebook which is just a fraction of traditional media advertising cost, but yet, has the potential of reaching thousands to millions of audiences across the globe. The new concept which is based on indirect marketing is taking advantage of social relations among family and friends, to circulate messages, by moving away from the traditional direct marketing, but employing old styled word-of-mouth communication style. Facebook understands that people rely on family and friends for recommendations when making a choice of products and services to buy. These trust based recommendations are considered valuable. Facebook makes good use of this to help users when their business goal is to reach a target or specific audience. It can also help you reach all the people that matter most, when it comes to promoting your business or your social event.

While the above statements may be true, businesses still need to follow some basic guidelines in order to make this new marketing concept work for them. Experts recommend steps for successful marketing with Facebook:

1. **Set up your page on Facebook**.
   Facebook page is a place to tell your story, and it is the center of every business you conduct on Facebook. Your Facebook Page helps people discover your business when they search. It also helps you get connected and have one-on-one conversations with your customers or fans who have come to like your page, read your posts and share them with friends. Your page can also help you reach large groups of people frequently, with messages tailored to their needs and interests. Your Facebook page is considered an extension of your business as it engages your customers on both desktop and their mobile devices. It has become an easy way to share updates. For instant activities reports, built-in analytics on your page will give you a deeper understanding of your customers and your marketing activities, through *Page Insights*.

   When you set up your page, Facebook automatically gives an URL that has a bunch of numbers. However, you can request page name with a web address that is similar to https://www.facebook.com/kommoacademy, which is easier to find. Topics about Facebook pages were discussed in details on chapter 6.

2. Identify your audience

Think about who you would like to meet in real life or offline to introduce your business to. With Facebook, you can reach the specific people who are most likely to become your customers. Your potential or ideal customers may have something in common such as age range, gender, or geographical location. Think about how your products or services can help each group. To build your audience, encourage your current customers and supporters to like your page. They are the people most likely to see your posts in their News Feed. Invite your friends and let the people in your life also know about your page so they can support you by liking it. This initial audience helps you establish credibility and spread the word about your offerings. Be your own spokesperson by liking your own page and sharing it as well. Though it is not much about the number of likes, but inviting your business contacts by uploading a list to send an email is recommended. It is important that you genuinely connect with your audience and engage with them on Facebook, as doing so will compel them to tell your story to their friends and fans.

3. Create compelling content

The secret of your success on Facebook marketing is to create page posts and ads that are interesting and valuable to your customers and to target your messages so the right people see them. When people like a post, comment on it, or share the post you created on your page, it appears on their friends' News Feed. When you notice that a post is getting a lot of engagement, promote it to reach even more people. Making successful posts into successful promotions is ideal for success.

4. Advertise on Facebook

Connect with new customers using the Ads you have designed to target potential customers, by their location, age, interest, gender, etc. These are the people that would like to hear from you again; people you can turn into repeat customers. It will demonstrate that "Like" is not just a button but someone who wants to stay in touch.

Facebook, as the social network giant, has become universally recognized as an excellent way to stay in touch with people. Its powerful advertising platform with sophisticated targeting options and easy integration with applications and pages makes it an interesting tool for individuals and marketers alike. One of such benefits of this giant social network is that anyone can place an Ad for the entire world to see. This new capability is a move away from the early days of advertising on Facebook where students used it as means of reaching other students to sell old textbooks or finding new roommates. Now that the site is open to the public, an Ad placed on Facebook can reach millions of people in a matter of seconds. In addition, Facebook has the granularity of tapping into each user's friends, and friends of friends, for ads based on their social behaviors or their likes. **Facebook Ads** are paid messages coming from businesses and they can include social context about friends. They are designed as a self service or do it yourself application that you can complete in a very short time. You can create an ad and choose when to run it, and people to target, but it will cost some small amount of money depending on the level of ad chosen. Reaching the right people is the key to marketing success; therefore, it is optimal to connect with people who are the right fit for your business using Facebook Ads. Statistics show that people who like your page spend an average of 2 times more as your customers than people who are not connected to you on Facebook. Therefore creating a page with content that will attract fans will make an ad more successful. There are many kinds or categories of ad a user or a business can choose from when running an ad campaign. Each comes with unique features and your budget will determine your choice. The most basic and inexpensive of all is the Social Ad.

Social ad is announcement a user can broadcast to specific Facebook market segment, such as men of certain age, women with college degrees, or working class people at the Microsoft Corporation. Social ads are usually designed as combination of graphic and text, and they usually pop up in the right hand side of the screen (Facebook ad space) or in people's News Feeds, or both, depending on how much the advertiser pays for the ads. More information can be found at https://www.facebook.com/business/connect for new Facebook marketers. Below are some tips on Facebook ads success:

   a. Focus on target audience – you will rely on your fan page *Like* to advance your campaign, therefore, your ads will show that your audience is most likely to "Like" your page.
   b. Add attention-getting Image – the image you use for your cover page is the key to getting your prospective fans attention. It is the image that will draw them to your ad so that they can read your headline and text.
   c. Create a logical headline - The headline of your ad should help to establish relevance and interest to your prospective fans. A logical headline should be short and to the point.
   d. Appropriate call to action – an ad is usually concluded by call to action which occurs in the text section of the ad.

5. **Measure and adjust.** How fans are engaged with Facebook page is measured by number of likes shares, and comments. Finding out what is working using some measurement tools is an ideal for determining your fans' inclination, so you can maximize the impact of every post and advertisement. Facebook has different tools to help you measure your progress. One of the handy tools is the Insights, which helps you to check for trends so you can develop more of the compelling content. Use Page Insights to understand who responds to your messages. This tool which displays graphs and numbers helps you understand the statistics based on gender, age, and location of the people who are the most engaged with your business so you can continue to engage them through targeted ads and promoted posts.

6. Influence new customers through your fans. Whenever people Like or Comment on your page, it creates a story that their friends can see. By boosting your content with sponsored story, you influence friends of your fans. Customers do not have to take your words for it; they have the recommendations of friends they trust. You built your business for your customers, now it is time to grow your business with Facebook.

Creating Facebook ads: Step-By-Step

1. Advertise on Facebook

From the Facebook page, click the pull-down menu, then *Advertise on Facebook.*

2. Create an Ad

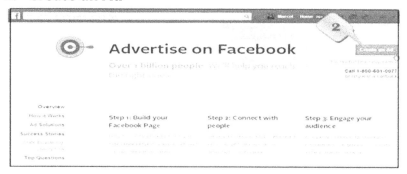

Then click the *Create an Ad* button of the "Advertise on Facebook" screen that appears.

3. Page Likes

Under "What kind of results do you want for your ads?", make a selection from the choices that appear. In this example, I selected *Page Likes.* Page likes helps you grow your audience on Facebook by displaying the ad on other users' ad space. When they click the like button, they become your fans - part of your new audience to receive future updates you post on the page. Other selections to choose from are, *Page Post Engagement* which create ads that boost your posts, increase your likes, comments, shares, video plays, and photo views. *Click to Website* is another choice that creates ads to encourage people to visit your website. Other advertisement types on the list are, *Website Conversions,App Installs, App engagement, Event Responses,* and *Offer Claims.* Each ad type is designed for specific end results, and exploring each to determine how it fits into you campaign is a good idea. In particular, *Event Responses,* which create ads to promote your event is worth looking into. Facebook Events App is popular among both businesses and individuals alike.

4. **Choose Page or Enter its URL**

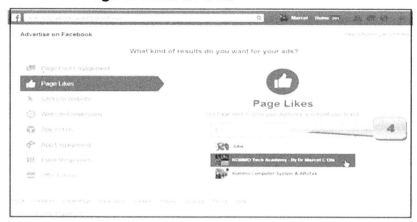

The above screen gives you the option to choose the page you like to promote from the pages listed, or just enter the page's address. In this example, the page titled "kommo Tech Academy ..." is listed and therefore selected.

5. **Create Images for the Ad**

You may use up to 6 different images to create ads in your campaign at no extra cost. Using this option, you can reach people who are not connected to your Page. It includes step by step approach that directs you to design your ad to include a headline, body text, and image. Get More Likes ads, encourage more people to like your Facebook Page with the above tool. The first image is automatically created with the cover page banner.

6. Audience Definition

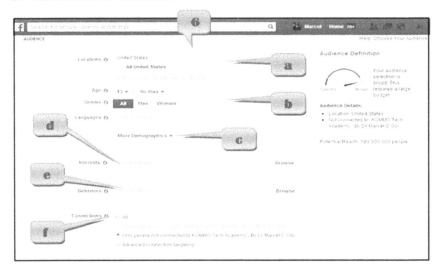

Your audience definition determines how much you are willing to spend on an ad. This plainly interpretes to, large audience – large budget, and small audience – small budget. (a) The default ad location is "all United States", but you can choose to exclude some areas. (b) The Age and Gender help you control the population in the area you like to reach. For instance, if you are promoting an adult film, you might want to bump the starting age to 18 instead of 13 which is the default. (c) More Demographics option gives you the option to chose from a wide variety of demographic audience including education (education level, fields of study, schools, years of college education), work (employers, industries, office type), financial (income, net-worth), home (household composition, home value, home ownership), ethnic affinity, generation, parents, politics, etc. (d) Interests let you choose from sports and technology to business and industry and everything in between. (e) Behaviors – purchase behavior, mobile device user, charitable donations, etc. (f) Connections gives you the option to promote to people not connected to your page; you may choose the "advanced connection targeting" to extend your ad to people who are already connected to your page, and friends of friends.

7. **Campaign and Ad Set**

This option uses the pre-set location and age range, but the budget can be adjusted here by setting the amount you are willing to spend on this ad campaign. In the above example, you can set the ad to run for $5.00 per day and on the schedule you can either run the ad contiously or choose "set a start and end date" to have more control over your ad.

8. **Bidding and Pricing**

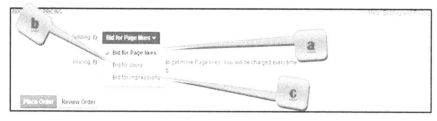

(a) *Bid for Page likes -* your bid will be optimized to get more Page likes. You will be charged every time someone is shown your ad.

(b) *Bid for clicks* - your bid will be optimized to get more clicks on your ad. You will be charged every time someone is shown your ad. You have the option to automatically optimize your bid to get more clicks or manually set your maximum bid for cost per click (CPC).

(c) **Bid for impressions** - you will be charged every time someone is shown your ad - $1.16 max. bid per 1,000 impressions

(d) **Place Order** – this authorizes Facebook to get payment from the credit card account you setup when signing up. Ads that run for a short period of time such as a month or less, are billed at the end of ad period.

Facebook closes the ad creation with this **warning** statement:

> By clicking "Place Order", you agree to the Facebook Statement of Rights and Responsibilities including your obligation to comply with the Facebook Advertising Guidelines. We do not use sensitive personal data for ad targeting. Topics you choose for targeting your ad don't reflect the personal beliefs, characteristics or values of users. Failure to comply with the Terms and Conditions and the Advertising Guidelines may result in a variety of consequences, including the cancellation of ads you have placed and the termination of your account. Understand that if you are a resident of or have your principal place of business in the US or Canada, you are contracting solely with Facebook, Inc. Otherwise, you are contracting solely with Facebook Ireland, Ltd.

Chapter 11

Facebook Mobile Integration

Facebook Mobile Overview

During the early stages of Facebook, it was only accessible via desktops and laptops. That was before it grew in popularity and became the number one social network in the world. Now, Facebook relies on mobile, devices especially cellular phones, in addition to its personal computer or pc base, for sustained market position and continued growth. Facebook is aware that its popularity is attributable, not only to its capability of connecting people, but also for the ability to allow users share information almost instantly. Facebook users want the same capability to connect no matter where they are in the world; they still want to be able to check friend's status updates, or to upload and share with friends, photos of the graduation party they attended, with or without their friends.

The social giant's thirst for mobile presence is evidenced by its recent acquisition of two prominent mobile social networks; Instagram and WhatsApp. With mobile tools, Facebook is making it easier and easier for people to communicate with cameras built into their cell phones and the associated apps. With mobile apps, you no longer have to go back to your PC or drag your laptop along everywhere you go, in order to upload photos or update statuses on Facebook. You can use Facebook mobile to constantly stay in touch with friends. Facebook mobile is also great for quick task – like looking up profile information and announcing your status updates.

Facebook is obviously improving its mobile user base. Cnet Reports that in U.S., more than 128 million people use Facebook Website on a daily basis, and that it also attracts 101 million people in the U.S. to its various mobile applications each day. The new stats on daily active users are part of a conscious effort by Facebook to more thoroughly educate advertisers on where they should spend their money. The reports added that Facebook daily visit of U.K. users is 24 million people, out of which 20 million people are Facebook mobile users. The social network's ability to continue to grow the number of people who come back on a daily basis has, in part, helped inspire renewed confidence in the value of its stocks.

Using Facebook Mobile

Facebook mobile is an app that allows you to use your Internet-ready mobile device to:

- **Upload photos and videos.** In today's information age where information needs to get out there before it becomes obsolete, posting photos and videos taken with cell phone is the fastest way to achieve this goal. With the cell phone, you can do this instantly without downloading first to your computer. Using your cell phone is truly the most convenient way to get it done.

- **Browse on your phone to interact with Facebook.** Facebook mobile web is a way to interact with Facebook using cell phones. You may use the touch screen or keypad to interact with your friends, just as you would use desktop computer or laptop. It helps you to do things such as updating your status, interact with your friend via chats and News Feed, and see updates on the events you have in your calendar and activities of your groups.

- **Use mobile text Feature.** The mobile text feature allows you to communicate with other users by text without using the web browser of your phone. It is faster than using web browser and can be used if you want to write a quick message on a friend's wall. A common practice is to text-message a friend with the friend's name. You can also receive text-messages on your phone if you sign up with text-message.

- **Subscribe to status updates.** You may use your mobile phone to subscribe for your friend's updates to receive updates each time they post new information, or update existing ones. The functionality is similar to web-based updates using desktop computer.

Setting up Facebook Mobile

Facebook mobile app installation is done differently, compared to other mobile apps. To install the mobile app, you start by associating your cellular phone number with your Facebook account in order to use it for mobile access. Facebook provides four simple steps to activate mobile phones to work with Facebook. The instructions for the mobile activation are described on the step-by-step shown below, under "how to activate your phone".

How to Activate Your Phone: Step-By-Step

1. Login to your Facebook account and click the account Gear located at the upper right corner of your page. In the dropdown menu that appears, click Account Settings.

2. Next, click the *Mobile* tab.

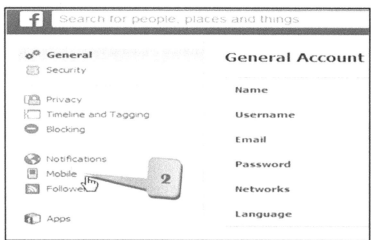

3. The Mobile tab displays on my Account page. Highlight the Mobile tab and click on "Register for Facebook text messages" link. Activate Facebook text (step 1 of 2) dialog box appears. Select country and mobile phone carrier and click next.

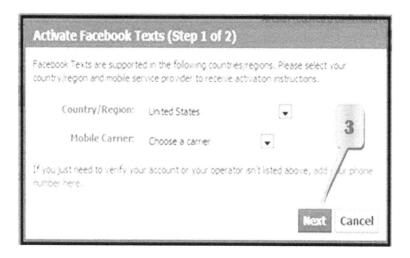

4. In (step 2 of 2) dialog box, send a text message from your phone with the letter "F" to the number 32665. Next, Facebook will respond by sending confirmation message to your mobile phone. Wait for the message to arrive (it may take longer than 5 minutes in some cases), then check your phone for the confirmation code which you will enter into the Facebook confirmation box to complete the activation. If the confirmation does not arrive within 15 minutes, you may have to repeat the text.

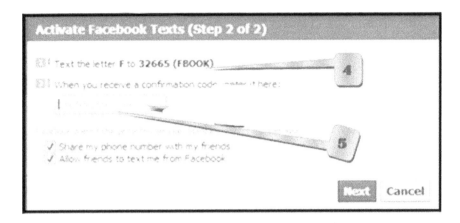

5. Once it arrives, enter your confirmation code into the step 2 of 2 dialog box input field. If you don't want your phone number made available to all your Facebook friends, leave the "Share my phone number with friends" checkbox unchecked, and then click next. At conclusion, you will receive messages on both your phone and e-mail. This will either indicate the code been accepted or rejected. Once you have successful activation and the code is accepted, you will be able to modify your mobile settings on Facebook.

Modifying Mobile Settings

It is highly recommended that you modify your Facebook mobile settings to customize it according to your preferences. This affects the type and number of messages you receive.

1. To modify your mobile settings, go to Facebook mobile page located at https://www.facebook.com/mobile. Facebook automatically displays the below page after completing the mobile activation process. On the page, click the account and choose account setting, then click the mobile tab.

2. Facebook Mobile Settings Page. On this page, you have the opportunity to remove the already added phone, add another mobile phone number, or activate Text Messaging for the existing one.

3. Once text messaging is activated, the mobile setting page appears with many configuration options.

Text Messaging - this defines the cellular phone number for Facebook to send you messages.

Facebook Messages – with this, you decide if you will accept mobile messages only from Facebook, or to also accept web-based messages.

Daily Text Limit – you can limit the maximum number of text message that will be sent your phone.

Post-By-Email Address – your post-by-email address is an email address you can use to upload photos or videos from your phone or regular e-mail system.

To find your post-by-email address:
    1. Click More Options under the status tool > Upload

Photo
2. Use the email address underneath Post it by email. Facebook advises that you don't share the email address with anyone since status updates or photos you send to it will be published directly onto your Facebook account.

Using your post-by-email address:
To add a caption to your photo or video, include a subject in the email. If you don't include any photos or videos, the email subject will be your updated status. Photos and videos uploaded by email are public by default, but you can always change the privacy setting of any photo album.

How to Use Facebook Mobile

Facebook Mobile interface allows you to add more than one mobile phone. However, after activating at least one phone, and modifying your preferences, it is ready for use.

Login to Facebook from your phone. With your mobile phone you may browse to http://m.facebook.com to access the scaled down mobile version. It will require your regular account name and other login information. An optimized version for iPhone users can be found at http://iphone.facebook.com.

Using cellular phone, you can do almost everything you do with computer when using Facebook. The list below contains the most popular thing you can do …
- Searching for people
- Tracking events
- Viewing photos
- Viewing statuses
- Uploading photos and videos
- Viewing news feeds.

Facebook – Mobile text Messaging

Some of the things you can do on Facebook such as sending a message to someone, or updating a status are also possible using Facebook cell phone texting. But, to achieve some of it or accomplish routine tasks, you have to text 32665 with predefined code and the message you wish to send. For instance, to delete your last status update, use the code "undo" with the message, "undo". To Search for an individual; use the code "search" with the message, "search", and the individual's name.

Table of Index

About the Author

Dr. Marcel C. Obi is an IT Professional with a Los Angeles County Government Department of the United States of America. Dr. Obi has over sixteen years of experience in general computing and served as the Department's Webmaster for over 8 years. His other responsibilities include Data Center Administration, Information Security, Electronic Mail Administration, and Web Development. He has more than six years of experience in Social Media development; with special emphasis on businesses/people integration. Areas of Social Media specialization include Facebook, Twitter, Linked In, and Nixle.

Dr. Marcel Obi has a Ph.D. degree in Information Systems from the Graduate School of Computer and Information Sciences, Nova Southeastern University, Fort Lauderdale, Florida. In addition, he has Bachelor of Business Administration degree in Marketing and MBA in Finance from the University of Central Oklahoma. He earned several IT certifications including Certified Information Security Manager (CISM), Certified Novell Engineer (CNE), and Microsoft Certified Professional (MCP). Dr. Obi is a renowned social media marketer, and has contributed to the wealth of knowledge of the cyberspace via video training and electronic books or eBooks.

www.ingramcontent.com/pod-product-compliance
Lightning Source LLC
Chambersburg PA
CBHW052147070326

40689CB00050B/2342